KEY CONCEPTS IN BUSINE
RESEARCH METHODS

Palgrave Key Concepts

Palgrave Key Concepts provide an accessible and comprehensive range of subject glossaries at undergraduate level. They are the ideal companion to a standard textbook making them invaluable reading to students throughout their course of study and especially useful as a revision aid.

Key Concepts in Accounting and Finance
Key Concepts in Bilingualism
Key Concepts in Business and Management Research Methods
Key Concepts in Business Practice
Key Concepts in Criminology and Criminal Justice
Key Concepts in Cultural Studies
Key Concepts in Drama and Performance (second edition)
Key Concepts in e-Commerce
Key Concepts in Human Resource Management
Key Concepts in Information and Communication Technology
Key Concepts in Innovation
Key Concepts in International Business
Key Concepts in Language and Linguistics (second edition)
Key Concepts in Law (second edition)
Key Concepts in Leisure
Key Concepts in Management
Key Concepts in Marketing
Key Concepts in Operations Management
Key Concepts in Philosophy
Key Concepts in Politics
Key Concepts in Public Relations
Key Concepts in Psychology
Key Concepts in Second Language Acquisition
Key Concepts in Social Research Methods
Key Concepts in Sociology
Key Concepts in Strategic Management
Key Concepts in Tourism

Palgrave Key Concepts: Literature
General Editor: Martin Coyle

Key Concepts in Contemporary Literature
Key Concepts in Creative Writing
Key Concepts in Crime Fiction
Key Concepts in Medieval Literature
Key Concepts in Modernist Literature
Key Concepts in Postcolonial Literature
Key Concepts in Renaissance Literature
Key Concepts in Romantic Literature
Key Concepts in Victorian Literature
Literary Terms and Criticism (third edition)

Further titles are in preparation

**Palgrave Key Concepts
Series Standing Order
ISBN 1–4039–3210–7**

(outside North America only)

You can receive future titles in this series as they are published by placing a standing order. Please contact your bookseller or, in the case of difficulty, write to us at the address below with your name and address, the title of the series and the ISBN quoted above.

Customer Services Department, Macmillan Distribution Ltd
Houndmills, Basingstoke, Hampshire RG21 6XS, England

Key Concepts in Business and Management Research Methods

Peter Stokes

First published 2011 by
PALGRAVE MACMILLAN

Palgrave Macmillan in the UK is an imprint of Macmillan Publishers Limited,
registered in England, company number 785998, of Houndmills, Basingstoke,
Hampshire RG21 6XS

Palgrave Macmillan in the US is a division of St Martin's Press LLC,
175 Fifth Avenue, New York, NY 10010.

Palgrave Macmillan is the global academic imprint of the above companies
and has companies and representatives throughout the world.

Palgrave® and Macmillan® are registered trademarks in the United States,
the United Kingdom, Europe and other countries.

ISBN: 978–0–230–25033–8

This book is printed on paper suitable for recycling and made from fully
managed and sustained forest sources. Logging, pulping and manufacturing
processes are expected to conform to the environmental regulations of the
country of origin.

A catalogue record for this book is available from the British Library.

A catalog record for this book is available from the Library of Congress.

10 9 8 7 6 5 4 3 2 1
20 19 18 17 16 15 14 13 12 11

Printed and bound in Great Britain by
CPI Antony Rowe, Chippenham and Eastbourne

Wishing Emma, Joel, Ellie, family and friends, health, happiness, laughter and the self-knowledge to realize what these truly are and when they have them.

And to Joseph Lemm (Machine Gun Corps) 20 May 1917 and Myer Goldberg (49 Squadron, RAF) 22/23 May 1944 who did not return and remain in 'some corner of a foreign field'.

לזכור   (Remember)

Contents

Acknowledgements

I have been thinking about writing this book for some time and I am very happy it is now done.

I would like to thank a number of people who caused it to happen and made it possible. Many thanks to Martin Drewe and Suzannah Burywood, my publishers at Palgrave Macmillan who provided me with the chance and brought it to fruition with drive, wise counsel and good humour. Thanks also to Ceri Griffiths, Jennifer Schmidt, Bryony Allen and Della Oliver who did so much to keep the book on the move and who were always so helpful and welcoming.

I cannot forget of course the many students (home and international) I have taught in the United Kingdom together with the students in Lyon and Amiens. All of them educated me so much through their curiosity and challenges. There are truly some remarkable and insightful people in the world. I hope this book is a response to their needs and frustrations and that it does justice to their questions.

Finally to my wife Emma and my children, Joel and Ellie, who, over some ten years have grown from saying 'luk, ahh daddy doin his "Hd" on the puter' to asking 'Dad, just how long are you going to be on the computer?'

PROFESSOR PETER STOKES
Chester Business School
University of Chester

Introduction

Materials and texts concerning **research methodology** and **research methods** have expanded rapidly in recent decades. A literature that once constituted only a handful of well-known generalist books has become a growing body of publications. A number of these texts contain helpful glossaries at the rear of the work. These provide students with brief and quick reference insights to key terms. This is valuable, but the present text, while working on a broadly similar principle, goes further.

Within the growing body of writing on research methodology, its diverse niches and aspects are gradually being identified and elaborated. This has been accompanied by a commensurate growth in journals of **research** as a signal of the development including, among others: *Qualitative Research in Organizations and Management, Action Research, Organizational Research Methods, Journal of Mixed Methods Research, Qualitative Research,* and *Qualitative Inquiry*. In spite of this welcome development in texts and materials, many students still find working their way through various readings and sources a challenge. Research methodology often seems to a confusing mix of 'isms' and 'ologies' and there is therefore scope for a text that provides support to the existing works on methodology. The aim of this text is to furnish students with an initial insight and commentary on common terms. It does not seek to provide a comprehensive or detailed portrayal of the terms; rather it seeks to provide some key points that will be helpful to somebody embarking on research, often for the first time. Moreover, in relation to students setting out to conduct research (be it for a proposal, dissertation or thesis), the suggestions in the present text should be followed in conjunction with any rules and regulations indicated and required by their own institutions.

The book is structured as a series of alphabetically organized entries, each followed by key words and useful references that afford the opportunity for follow-up reading or that illustrate the term in context. Within the entries, words appearing as entries elsewhere in the book are highlighted in bold. In this way, the text operates in an interconnected manner with each term informing and cross-refer-encing a series of others in the work. It is hoped that readers will find the text easy to read and understand and that it will provide them with an interest and appetite to learn more about the fascinating area of research methods and methodology.

PROFESSOR PETER STOKES
Chester Business School
University of Chester

Abstract

An abstract is a short statement that aims to summarize the key points of a piece of **research**. These points comprise: the background context of the paper; the aim of the research; the literature in which it is grounded; the **research methods** and **methodologies** employed to gather and analyse data; the key findings and conclusions; and often Key Words associated with the research. In essence, it is a cameo or overview of the entire work. It allows the reader to rapidly peruse the contents, form and outcome of the research in order to determine whether it might be useful to the information search being undertaken. Importantly, it should be noted that the abstract is different to an **introduction**. For instance, prefaces and introductions open the window on the work but do not offer closure or reveal the ending and findings. This function is carried out by the **discussion** and conclusion of the given text in conjunction with the introduction. In contrast, an abstract briefly tells the reader the beginning, the middle and the end or outcome of the paper's study, **argument** and purpose.

The abstract is positioned at the front of a piece of work. Journal articles, **dissertations** and **theses** tend to have abstracts. In a journal article, the abstract will be on the front page situated just after the **title**. In dissertations and theses, the abstract will appear on pages soon after the title. Books do not usually have abstracts and tend instead to have prefaces and/or introductions, which, as outlined above, are not the same as abstracts.

Abstracts can vary in length but will generally be short. Often there will be guidelines in the journal or, if it is for a dissertation or **thesis**, in the institutional guidelines or student handbook. A typical length will range between approximately 300 and 500 words. The abstract will not be page numbered like the pages of the main body of the text. Often the abstract, contents and other early pages in a work may use Roman numerals (that is, i, ii, iii, iv and so on and so forth) whereas the main body of text will employ Arabic numerals (that is, 1, 2, 3 and so on). An abstract will not necessarily use References (see **referencing**).

Although not the same, there are arguably parallels between an abstract and the idea of the executive summary of a report. Its purpose is to allow the reader to glean a rapid and broad insight into the document. However, it should be noted that an executive summary will indicate recommendations stemming from the report and will be written in business English for an executive audience.

Key Words
Article, Dissertation, Introduction, Paper, Summary, Thesis

References
Quinton and Smallbone (2006); Wilson (2010)

Access

Access concerns the right to have admittance to – and to gain **knowledge** of – a particular domain, area or document. The granting of access is dependent on the co-operation and collaboration of the people whom you wish to talk to or observe, that is, prospective **respondents.** This will frequently involve a process of telephone, letter correspondence and face-to-face negotiation.

Achieving successful access will depend on a significant number of factors, including, for example, that the **research questions** need to be of interest to the respondents; the **researcher** needs to exhibit credibility; the research questions need to be mindful of sensitivities of the respondents and the **research** setting (paraphrased from: Hair, Money, Samouel and Page (2007: 75–8).

In addition, access will often also involve a need to gain ethical approval from relevant bodies for the study in order to ensure that proposed respondents are not exposed to harm in any form, be it bodily or to their privacy or reputation (see **ethics**).

A

The actual skills required to attain access can be likened, in some ways, to being a sales person. Sometimes access will need to be made through 'cold' contacts (that is, people you have never spoken to before) and sometimes through 'warm' contacts, that is, contacts that have come as referrals from previous contacts.

Key Words
Ethics, Research, Respondents

References
Hair, Money, Samouel and Page (2007)

Action Research

Action Research is an approach wherein the **researcher** conducts **research** in a given client setting in collaboration with a person or group who live and/or work at the researched location (Cooke and Wolfram Cox, 2005). The **objective** of the research is to bring about a change and research outcome that will be deemed useful to the client organization. Eden and Huxham (1996: 75) have stated that the issue under investigation must be of 'genuine concern' to the people working in the organization or research setting and not solely of interest to the researcher(s). In other words, clients will want to feel that in undertaking the collaborative research with academics they are addressing 'real world' issues and problems. An Action Research approach contrasts with, for example, a research project where the researcher gathers **data** at a research site almost separately or independently of the people based at the research location. This 'distancing' continues as the researcher(s) goes on to write up the research and then publishes in an outlet such as, for example, a journal, which potentially is of little interest to the research **respondents.** Although not always the case, this latter process, it can be argued, has little or no useful consequences for the researched community.

This raises concerns for many academics, as research is not always seen as having much direct benefit for those people subjected to the research. Researchers can be seen as people who appear, gather data and simply leave, never to be seen or heard of again. Action Research is concerned about solving real problems and situations in organizations. This means that there may well be a degree of unpredictability in the way the research develops. This may also mean departing, to some extent, from the originally discussed aims of the research in order to take account of some related or consequential development. Equally, Action Research implies that things are likely to change in the research location. Employees or organizational members may begin to think differently about certain matters as a result of the intervention. In this way, the Action Research has an interactive and a dynamic dimension to it.

Researchers involved in Action Research are likely, but not always of course, to be involved in some form of **participant observation** role. They will be completely familiar with and immersed in the organization. This means they have the difficult task of leading the 'double-life' of being seen as 'researcher looking at the organization' at the same time as being seen by many as 'part of the organization' and the inherent organizational politics.

Action Research is often considered to have its roots in the work of, among others, the applied psychologist Kurt Lewin (1890–1947). However, commentary and variations on this approach have become so diverse over recent decades that identifying one definition or a single theoretical approach is very challenging (see Reason and Bradbury, 2001). Due, in part, to a diversity of traditions at play, Action Research can throw up challenges for particular methodological approaches (see Eriksson and Kovalainen, 2008: 193–209 for further guidelines).

Key Words
Participant Observation, Real Problems, Collaborative Research

References
Cooke and Wolfram Cox (2005); Eden and Huxham (1996); Eriksson and Kovalainen (2008); Reason and Bradbury (2001)

Active Response Rate

The active response rate, also referred to occasionally as the *response rate*, is a way of measuring the success rate of **data collection** in a piece of **research**. Simply stated, response rate is how many people actually replied to or participated in the research. These **data** will usually be collected through a range of well-known possible **research methods** including, by way of illustration, interviews or questionnaires of various types, **focus groups**, surveys and so on and so forth (see **survey research**).

There is an underlying more technical definition of response rate (because we need to take account of people in the sample who, for whatever reason, have not played a part in the research) and this is:

Total number of responses ÷ total number of **respondents***
in the sample* (excluding invalid and impossible to contact/
reach respondents)
(*See entries for **respondents** and **sampling**)

A

There might be a range of reasons why certain respondents have not been included in a research project ranging from respondents straightforwardly declining to be involved to an inability to identify or find the respondent. Equally, some responses might be invalid if, for example, the respondent has given confusing responses or, alternatively, shown the research was not being taken seriously. It is important to exclude these returns from the total number of respondents figure, otherwise, when the active response rate is calculated, it will produce an inaccurate result.

Generally speaking, the higher the response rate the more convincing is the coverage of the research, and hence representative of the issues under examination in the study. However, this may be more of a concern in studies employing random **sampling**. This is because a random sample expressly aims to have representativeness as an **objective**. Many studies, especially in the field of business, management and organization research, often use non-random, small convenience samples that would never make any claim to being representative of a given category or domain. It is important to be clear that while small samples do not prevent the authors from making worthwhile observations, they do mean that it is difficult, if not impossible, to generalize the findings very far and therefore further research and studies are often called for.

Key Words
Random Sampling, Representativeness, Respondent

References
Jankowicz (2005); Saunders, Lewis and Thornhill (2007)

Aim

A

An aim is a point, purpose or outcome that is sought to be achieved or accomplished. The term *aim* is most commonly used in documents such as **dissertations**, projects or **theses**. An aim indicates what the work is setting out to do in the broadest sense possible. Indeed, the aims often resemble the **title** of the work.

Aims are often followed and qualified by a subset of **objectives.** Whereas aims point at the general and overall intent of the work, objectives will usually indicate the step-by-step phases or tasks that will need to be undertaken in order to achieve the aim. Interestingly, many **research methodology** texts do not generally discuss aims in any detail, seemingly taking it for granted that this will be a commonly understood term (however, see Wilson, 2010: 46–9 for a useful and practical exposition). Nevertheless, as indicated above, it is important to be clear about how the aims differ from objectives. Aims have been commented on to a large extent in other organization and management fields such as, for instance, strategy.

Key Words
Intent, Objectives, Strategy

References
Wilson (2010)

Analysis

The term *analysis* describes the process whereby, for example, **data**, a subject area or domain is examined in detail in order to better understand it. This process is likely to involve the breaking down or categorization of the area under scrutiny into manageable or understandable units or groupings. In doing this, the intention is to allow complex issues and problems to be presented and considered in a more simplified manner.

The **method** of analysis will need to be complementary to, and fit within, the overall methodological, philosophical, epistemological and ontological position used in the **research** work (see **research methodology**, **epistemology** and **ontology**). This could take many forms including, for example: **interpretivism, postmodernism, poststructuralism, critical realism, deconstructionism** and so on and so forth (see by way of illustration Boje's (2001: 15–16) tabulation of these positions in relation to methodological analytical approaches and the use of **storytelling** in research).

In the main, the analytical approaches will tend to adhere to what are broadly termed either an inductive or deductive way of making sense of the data (see **inductivism, deductivism** and **sensemaking**). For example, approaches such as interpretivism, postmodernism and poststructuralism will tend to take a broadly inductive approach to analytical activities (see **inductivism**). If the **researcher** is using an inductive approach then the analysis will tend to be **iterative,** emergent and incremental and will involve processes of looking over these data in order to try to identify patterns, recurrent terms and salient features. This will, of course,

A

rely on the analytical expertise of the researcher and his or her ability to listen, observe and record what **respondents** are saying and doing. In inductivism, this does not mean that these data will be subsequently analysed or perceived in an objective manner (see **objectivity**). On the contrary, an inductive approach means the analysis acknowledges and accepts that **subjectivity** plays an important role in the way people make sense of and socially construct (or indeed deconstruct) their world(s) (see **sense-making, social constructionism** and **Weltanschauung**). In an inductive **frame of reference**, the researcher is inextricably involved in these subjective processes and will be most likely to write overtly about them in his or her research accounts (see **reflexivity** and **subjectivity**).

Alternatively, the researcher might choose, or be persuaded, to adopt a positivistic or post-positivistic stance which would be based in a deductive approach to the analysis and overall piece of research (see **positivism** and **deductivism**). In these methodological stances, the research and analysis conducted therein will aim to achieve **objectivity** and a lack of **bias**. This will commonly be sought by employing in the research what the researcher believes to be only incontrovertible and independently verifiable facts, figures and observations. Opinions, beliefs, expressions of interest and suppositions are likely to be discounted from the analysis. Of course, what has been mapped out above is a broad indication of an inductive–deductive spectrum. Nevertheless, within this, a key factor to take account of in analysis is the stance of the researcher in relation to the corresponding subjectivity–objectivity belief axis discussed above.

On a final, more operational and practical, note useful guideline questions that a researcher might consider when carrying out analysis might include:

- How should you organize your data?
- How to hear what your data has to say?
- How to recognize and pattern your own ideas about the data?
- How to organize evidence for your interpretation?
- How to present your findings?
- How and what techniques to select?

(Adapted from Riley, 1990)

A

Key Words
Deductivism, Frame of Reference, Inductivism, Interpretivism, Objectivity, Subjectivity

References
Boje (2001); Riley (1990)

Anonymity

The term *anonymity* is linked to the word 'anonymous'. It is derived from Greek and signifies 'nameless'. In **research**, anonymity is concerned with the process of not disclosing or revealing the name or identity of a person or entity (for example a company or institution) that has been accessed or played a role in the research. This is a very important ethical principle for much research (see **ethics**) as it ensures that no third party can read the research and do harm (deliberately or inadvertently), through embarrassment or to somebody's or some entity's reputation.

Moreover, it is important to appreciate that some research **respondents** may very well expressly desire for their name to be associated and stated in the write-up of the research. This may even be the case if the research is to be published subsequently in a public domain. If the respondent (be it individual or organization) states that he or she does not mind being named in the research, it will still be useful to secure this in writing in either a letter or email in the event that questions or difficulties arise later. It is important to underline that such potential problems could even result in legal action against the **researcher** for libel and therefore it is vital not to underestimate the significance of decisions over anonymity.

Key Words
Confidentiality, Ethics, Harm, Reputation

References
Bryman and Bell (2007); Collis and Hussey (2009)

A

Appendix (*plural* Appendices)

In the **context** of a **research** document, an appendix is generally considered to be a section positioned at the rear of the document that contains supplementary and subsidiary material. The purpose of the appendix is to provide a space for **information** or documents that the author considers of value or interest but does not want to put them in the main body of the text. There may be a number of reasons for this. On the one hand, it might be that the information or document allocated to the appendix is full of detail, for example **statistics**, and to place it in the main body of the text would obscure or interfere with the flow of the argument. Nevertheless, the author(s) of the document believes that the document is a significant supporting part of the overall paper or **thesis** being presented and needs to be made available to the reader. Things that might be presented in an appendix include, for example, **questionnaires** relating to the study, statistical tables referred to the main text, and diagrams and images (Wilson, 2010: 288).

Appendices can be very useful. However, they should also be used sparingly and with caution. It is a common misunderstanding on the part of some students that the addition of a large appendix full of documents generally connected to the argument of the work will somehow add value to it or compensate for a weak main body of the work. When using an appendix, an important point to remember is that the material in the appendix needs to be directly discussed and referenced in the main body of the work. It is never acceptable or sufficient simply to append the appendix to the rear of the **dissertation** or thesis as if it were a separate body of information. Equally, appendices are not intended to be used as a means to get around word limits.

Key Words
Dissertation, Information, Statistics, Thesis

References
Wilson (2010)

Applied Research

A

Applied research is an approach that has the purpose of focusing on a particular problem with the objective of finding a solution to that problem. This may commonly be for a particular client or commercial project (the parallels with **Action Research** can be noted here). This approach contrasts, for example, with pure or theoretical types of **research** which may well examine and gather **data** from a physical environment or **respondent** but not directly seek to change anything within that setting (Easterby-Smith, Thorpe and Jackson, 2008). Rather, theoretical research, often in contrast to applied, aims to develop the theoretical framework and appreciations pertaining to a general domain rather than solving a specific problem in an immediate manner.

It is quite common for part-time students to undertake applied research in relation to their workplace. It should be pointed out that this can, on occasion, produce political tensions as the employer (often sponsoring the part-time student's programme to some greater or lesser extent) aims to guide or even commandeer the work entirely for the company's ends. This can be a difficulty because the research is also intended to be part of an academic process and award. Moreover, there is the possibility of applied research raising ethical tensions and issues. For example, applied research is very likely to be become involved with, and have consequences for, organizational members' positions, standing and identity.

Key Words
Politics, Problem, Solution

References
Easterby-Smith, Thorpe and Jackson (2008)

Archival Research

Archives are specially prepared storage areas for old documents and materials. Quite often these will be assembled in collections such as public records offices; see for example the National Archives located at Kew, Surrey (www.nationalarchives.gov.uk) or the British Library in Central London (www.bl.uk). When a **researcher** accesses and studies documents in such a place it is usually termed archival **research**. In addition, it is often the case that individual companies, organizations and institutions build and maintain archive collections that chart their own particular histories.

Archival research is commonly used in certain disciplines, for example history, and, in the case of organization and management, the area known as business history. Equally, however, it can be used as part of a **research design** in any subject domain providing rich and detailed secondary diachronic (that is, historical) and contemporary materials (see **data** for comments on *secondary data*).

Key Words
Documents, Secondary Research

References
www.bl.uk (2010); www.nationalarchives.gov.uk (2010); Wilson (2010)

Autoethnography

Autoethnography is an approach to **research** that allows the **researcher** to focus in an in-depth manner on his or her own feelings and thoughts in relation to the research field under investigation. It contrasts to some extent with **ethnography**. While ethnography takes account of the researcher/ participant observer, it has the **aim** of studying a group or community (rather than the researcher's emotions directly; see **participant observation**) (see Chang, 2008; Muncey, 2010; and in particular see the special issue on autoethnography of *Journal of Contemporary Ethnography* edited by Hunt and Ruiz Junco, 2006).

Autoethnography is becoming increasingly widely used in a range of subject areas including business, organization and management (Brewis, 2005; Ford and Harding, 2008).

Autoethnography often employs **data** in the form of narratives and stories, which can then be analysed and interpreted through various frameworks and conceptual structures (see **narrative research**). As an approach to research inquiry, autoethnography provokes some controversy with regard to its ability to offer **validity**, **reliability** and **generalizability**. These concerns tend to centre on the degree to which extensive **subjectivity** is likely to play a role in relation to the research, data, findings and interpretation, and extent to which this is considered a problem (see **inductivism** and **deductivism**). One typical technique used to address this issue is the cross-referencing or **triangulation** of the final research account with research **respondents** in similar or related situations. In other words, do these individuals recognize and acknowledge, to some greater or lesser point, the narrative and findings that have been produced? Moreover, the autoethnographer usually goes to considerable lengths to describe and portray their thought processes in as explicit and transparent manner as possible.

A

Key Words
Ethnography, Narrative Research, Storytelling

References
Brewis (2005); Chang (2008); Ford and Harding (2008); Hunt and Ruiz Junco (2006); Muncey (2010)

Axial Coding

Coding is the process whereby the categories are developed for the **data** that have been collected. There are various approaches to coding. Axial coding is a process that, through analysis, seeks to identify and build subcategories within main categories in the data. Software is available that can facilitate this process (for example NVivo) and may use terminology such as 'parent' and 'child' nodes (Eriksson and Kovalainen, 2008; Wilson, 2010).

Axial coding is often considered to fit into a sequence of open, axial and selective codings. Open coding (an initial identification and labelling of events, characters, occurrences in the raw data) leads on to axial coding (which refines this to some extent through the creation of groupings of related terms and subcategories within them). This is then followed by selective coding (which involves development of the bigger theoretical scheme), which forms part of the methodological approach known as **Grounded Theory** (Bryman, 2008; Saldaña, 2009).

Key Words
Analysis, Categories, Coding

References
Bryman (2008); Eriksson and Kovalainen (2008); Saldaña (2009); Wilson (2010)

A

Bar Chart

A bar chart is a form of diagram, or graph, in which **data** are represented by bars or columns. The columns, or bars, can be either vertical or horizontal. The chart shows the relationship between two **variables** (that is, is bivariate), one plotted on the horizontal axis and the other plotted on the vertical axis (Saunders, Lewis and Thornhill, 2007). For example, on the vertical access a given chart may show 'quantity of sales in pounds (£)' and on the horizontal axis different supermarkets may be sequentially listed. By looking at the different bar sizes on the chart, this would allow the reader to see the relative sizes of sales of the various organizations included. Therefore, to summarize, each column, or bar, in the graph stands for, or shows, a particular category in the data. The length, or size, of the columns is based on the count or the numbers of times pieces of data in that particular category occur. For example:

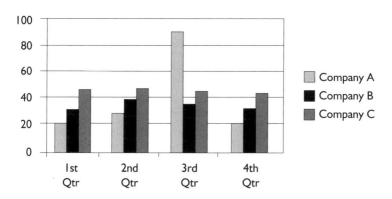

Figure 1 Bar chart showing sales in millions of pounds (£)

A bar chart should not be confused with a histogram. A **histogram** is different from a bar chart in that the *area* of the bars on a histogram reflects the value of the data being charted. Conversely, a bar chart is a simple and straightforward count of how many times (that is, the **frequency**) a particular value or piece of data (for example every pound of sales value) occurs. This means that on the horizontal axis of a histogram there will not be any space between the different blocks because this space will always form part of the area of one of the categories. This contrasts with a bar chart where there are likely to be spaces between bars on the chart (but not necessarily). These spaces do not have any significance in a bar chart but might assist in enhancing the clarity of the chart. Bar charts are sometimes seen as an alternative to **pie charts**.

Key Words
Axis, Data, Frequency, Variable

References
Ha (2011); Payne (2011); Saunders, Lewis and Thornhill (2007)

Behaviour Variables (*see* Variables)

Bias

Bias means giving emphasis to a particular viewpoint or perspective. This may on occasion take place due to prejudice or allotting undue stress on a particular point or position. This is an important concern for **research** where there is a powerful commitment to achieving results that can be considered as representative, truthful and meaningful. There are many possible instances of bias in research processes. By way of illustration, one example of the introduction of bias is where the interviewer leads the **respondent** or interviewee to skew or influence answers in a particular manner.

Nevertheless, situations such as the one outlined above may not be as clear-cut as first seems to be the case. In research processes, bias is inextricably linked to contesting ideas of **subjectivity** and **objectivity**. Within deductive, positivistic processes, objectivity, and the removal of any possible bias, is considered to be a central requirement in order to ensure the **validity** of the findings and conclusions (see **deductivism** and **positivism**).

On the other hand, methodological approaches that employ inductive, interpretivistic approaches tend to be open to the idea and

B

recognition that human interpretation and judgement, in other words some form of bias, are at play in research situations (see **inductivism** and **interpretivism**). Inductive approaches accord importance to the **sense-making** and constructive processes that are involved in using our perception and senses to see and interpret **data**. Clearly, inductive processes are as concerned about methodological issues of **reliability**, validity and **generalizability** as objectivity-espousing deductive processes. However, these are approached and accounted for differently under inductive approaches.

Key Words
Deductivism, Inductivism, Interpretivism, Objectivity, Positivism, Prejudice, Sense-making, Subjectivity

References
Alvesson and Sköldberg (2009)

B

Case Study

Within a **research** project, a case study is considered to be a research approach involving the in-depth study of a real-life entity or **context** having clearly outlined and definitive boundaries. A case study can use a range of **research methods** and sources in order to gather its information. Equally, it may involve **qualitative** and **quantitative data**. Typically (although, of course, not always) a case study will have the following layout: an **introduction**; background history leading up to the contemporary period or moment; the current situation and the focal issues or problems that are to be considered (this may or may not involve the development of a **hypothesis** or **hypotheses** to be answered); analysis of the issues; proposed solutions (Yin, 2002, 2011).

The use of case studies in business and management teaching and learning is a common practice. In particular, 'ready-made' case studies from textbooks, or case study archives, are well known to students on both undergraduate and postgraduate programmes. It is common practice to use a financial ratio analysis on the accounts or numbers contained in the case accompanied by a written commentary on the wider issues of the case. Indeed, in the early years, following the introduction of Master of Business Administration (MBA) programmes, it was a popular criticism that students on these courses tended to spend too much time working on case studies at the expense of direct experiential learning in organizational settings.

If electing to use case studies as part of your research, you may decide to develop data for a single case study or, alternatively, you may develop multiple case studies. Within the single case study, the intention is to carry out a detailed exploration of the issues, themes and patterns that occur within it and make comparisons between these in order to derive findings for **analysis**. In the case of a piece of research using multiple case studies, more usually than not, the **researcher's** intention is to develop insights by making comparisons and contrasts between the situations identified in the different case studies. This could follow myriad possibilities but, for example, it could involve research into several different companies to analyse how they have, each in their own way, implemented a latest quality initiative.

Key Words
Hypothesis, Single Case Study, Multiple Case Studies

References
Yin (2002, 2011)

Causality

Causality is the situation or condition where one event or situation is brought about by another earlier or preceding event. Causality is a central assumption underlying **research** using **experimental design** and the general approach to deductive research (see **deductivism**). It assumes that **variables** can be examined in isolation from other variables and the surrounding situation or context in order to see the effect that changes in one variable have on another (Maylor and Blackmon, 2005: 200–6). An example of this, among the many possible, might be to consider what changes in price (variable A) have on demand for a product (variable B).

   The restriction of a piece of research to such variables, and the attendant belief in the possibility of isolating them, might be critiqued, particularly by **researchers** who habitually use inductive approaches – see **inductivism**. Therein, causality is seen as oversimplifying the complexity and messiness of real-life situations. This, in turn, can mean that a wide range of contextual factors are marginalized or overlooked.

Key Words
Deductivism, Experimental Design, Inductivism, Variable

References
Maylor and Blackmon (2005)

C

Chi Square Test

This is a test to distinguish whether there is a statistical relationship between two **variables** (Jankowicz, 2005). Chi square tests are used in **quantitative**, **experimental design**, deductive type **research** (see **deductivism**). The test tends to be employed when a **researcher** has tabulated (that is, put **data** into a two by two table form) various categories of variable and wishes to see if any relationship can be identified between them.

Key Words
Deductivism, Experimental Design, Quantitative, Variable

References
Jankowicz (2005)

Closed Question

A closed question is a question that can logically provoke only a limited response, such as, for example 'yes' or 'no'. This might be needed or desirable for certain aspects of an **interview** or **questionnaire** where a simple answer is required. However, quite often a more elaborate and in-depth answer may be desired by the **researcher** and an **open question** that encourages the views and opinions of the **respondent** may be used (Bulmer, 2012; Remler and (Van) Ryzin, 2011).

An example of a closed question might be:

'Do you like your job?' (which tends to invite the possibility of a 'yes' or 'no' answer)

While the same issue asked as an open question might be:

'Please describe your thoughts and feelings about your job.'

Closed questions quite often allow the number of responses to be counted and represented in, for example, a **bar chart**.

Key Words
Interview, Open Question, Questionnaire, Respondent, Researcher

References
Bulmer (2012); Remler and Van Ryzin (2011)

Coding

Coding involves processes that lead to categorization and classification of **data** so that more detailed **analysis**, relationships and understandings can be established and discerned. Coding for **qualitative** data can encompass various approaches. As Maylor and Blackmon (2005) indicate, when it has been initially gathered, qualitative data tends to 'not [be] processed or transformed', 'take many forms', '[not be] standardized', '[be] voluminous'. In these instances, coding will involve looking over the data numerous times in order to establish patterns, shapes based on recurrent statements, **language**, images, metaphors, allusions and so on and so forth. Each of these occurrences might then be ascribed a code indicating that the particular mention in the data shows it belongs to a particular group or category. In this way, the **researcher** begins to build an impression of how the **respondents** understand or develop **meaning** in relation to their world and the **research** environment or setting.

Grounded Theory is a particular approach to analysing and coding qualitative data. This is an involved and complex process that has generated a substantial body of literature. Many research projects state that they are using Grounded Theory when in fact they are not. Rather they are using a limited number of the practices and processes that go to make up a Grounded Theory approach (also see **axial coding**) (Maylor and Blackmon, 2005).

For **quantitative** data, it is common practice to use a statistically based approach that will show where correlations and statistically significant relationships exist or not (see **correlation** and **statistics**). This, in turn, allows patterns and sequences in the data to be determined. The analysis and coding of both qualitative and quantitative data can be undertaken manually or by using software such as SPSS (Wilson, 2010).

Key Words
Analysis, Data, Grounded Theory, Qualitative, Quantitative, Researcher, Respondents

References
Maylor and Blackmon (2005); Wilson (2010)

Cognitive Mapping

Cognitive mapping is an approach that allows a **researcher** or team of researchers to chart issues and ideas and develop constructs visually. The process usually involves an initial phase of 'dumping' or generating **data** on a given topic, issue or question. Subsequent phases involve clustering and shaping the data in relation to key ideas and **objectives.**

Within business and management, cognitive mapping is an approach that tends to be employed in relation to strategy formulation (see Ackermann, Eden and Brown, 2005), however, there is extensive scope to consider using the approach as a means of better understanding the issues at play in a given **research** setting or project. Cognitive mapping can also be very helpful in charting and identifying the interconnections of the emergent themes in bodies of literature during **literature reviews.**

Key Words
Data, Literature Review

References
Ackermann, Eden and Brown (2005)

Concept

A concept is a theoretical idea or notion on a given topic. Concepts are conceived from, and in relation to, research **data** and the development of concepts forms an important aspect of the **research** process.

It is common to talk about the 'conceptual framework' of a study or piece of work. This remark points at the philosophical ideas and constructs that the work uses to direct the design of study, the **analysis** employed and the **meaning** discerned and conclusions achieved. In other words the conceptual framework is the set of overarching ideas that underpin the research (Clegg, Kornberger and Pitsis, 2008).

Key Words
Data, Idea

References
Clegg, Kornberger and Pitsis (2011)

Confidentiality

Confidentiality concerns keeping a secret or not disclosing information obtained from a particular person or source to a third party. This is a very important principle in **research**. More often than not a research project will involve gathering **data** from a range of people and sources through **research methods** such as **interviews** and **questionnaires**. When **respondents** supply information to a research project it will often be on the explicit, and even implicit, understanding that the information will not have their name stated in connection with it. In other words, it will often be anonymized (see **anonymity**)(Gill and Johnson, 2010: 160). Such an understanding or agreement is likely to form a mutually negotiated condition of the research before the project commences. For data that need to be kept confidential, the **researcher(s)** needs to put in place a plan at the beginning of the research stating where the data will be kept and secured, for how long, and what will happen to the data (and when) once the project has been completed.

Confidentiality is an important aspect of the **ethics** surrounding a piece of research and will be mentioned in any ethical statements connected with a research project (Israel and Hay, 2006: 77–94). Many organizations and institutions, especially universities, have bodies such as ethics committees who have overview of proposed research and the powers of veto on the progression of a research project if terms of confidentiality or related provisions are in question or have been breached.

Key Words
Agreement, Anonymity, Data, Ethics, Respondents

References
Gill and Johnson (2010); Israel and Hay (2006)

C

Consent

Consent involves giving agreement or permission for something to take place or happen. This also usually implies that consent was freely given rather than as a consequence of any force or manipulation being exercised.

Two main forms of consent – positive consent and negative consent – are worth noting in relation to **research** projects. Positive consent is where the **respondents** are explicitly asked by the **researcher** for permission (usually written and signed) to conduct the research with, and gather **data** from, them. This is by far the normal and usual practice. Alternatively, negative consent is where the potential respondent is informed about the impending research and is given the option to withdraw before it commences. If he or she does not indicate his or her withdrawal prior to the research commencing then the research team make the assumption that they will be included. In research projects taking place in the contemporary era, negative research is rarely used because it is difficult to defend on ethical grounds (see **ethics**). However, forms of it can still sometimes be seen in, for example, workplace surveys conducted internally. It could be argued that the very term *negative consent* is a tautology (that is, a contradiction in terms) because how can a person consent *negatively*?

Informed consent is also employed as a term meaning that participants indicate they are willing to engage in a project. As Fisher (2010: 64–7) indicates this is often *implied*, by actions such as participants just going ahead and completing a questionnaire. However, it is usually preferable to get participants *explicitly* to complete a consent form before asking them to do anything (see Fisher, mentioned above, for an interesting example of a consent form).

Key Words
Agreement, Ethics, Negative Consent, Permission, Positive Consent

References
Fisher (2010)

Constant Comparison

This is a process of data **analysis** used in inductive **research** processes (see **inductivism**). These **data** will usually be contained in a range of places, for example documents, **interview** transcripts and **participant observation** notes (see **transcription**). Constant comparison aims to identify events, statements, **language**, expressions and so on in these recordings and documents in order to ascertain patterns, trends and recurrent situations. This allows the **researcher** to see emergent themes and **concepts** from the data analysis. A central idea behind constant comparison is the attempt to keep the generation of **theory** and theoretical constructs closely related to the original data. Also, under constant comparison, as data analysis progresses and theoretical ideas emerge, the researcher feeds the theory back into the data and, reciprocally, runs new data through already established theory.

Constant comparison is often discussed in association with **Grounded Theory** (Charmaz, 2006; Goulding, 2002; Strauss and Corbin, 1998) although increasingly it is a process discussed and employed more within **qualitative** approaches to research.

Key Words
Analysis, Concepts, Data, Grounded Theory, Inductivism, Theory

References
Charmaz (2006); Goulding (2002); Strauss and Corbin (1998)

Constructionism (*also termed* Constructivism)

Constructionism is a belief that people, through the course of their everyday interactions in many different situations, create much of what comes to be perceived as reality or realities. It is an ontological position that some **researchers** choose to adopt in their approach to designing and analysing **research** (see **ontology** and **analysis**) (Eriksson and Kovalainen, 2008).

Constructionism is based on a number of assumptions. Firstly, that the labelling of objects and events (otherwise termed **representation**) is *not a pre-given* 'fact'. Rather events and their representation are the products and outcomes of social interaction between people. Groups of people and communities develop and decide what is important and significant to them and attribute names to things and events as part of this process. In other words, events and situations are made or produced by the human gaze and by human definition – they do not pre-exist as such. This is not to say that objects do not, and did not, exist before humans appeared on the earth. Mountains, rain, meadows, storms and eclipses *exist*. Equally, so do human created objects such as houses and roads. However, human **sense-making** processes develop (or alternatively, construct) meaning, labelling, folklore, categorization, understanding, learning and so on and so forth in relation to these objects and moments (Watson and Harris, 1999). Moreover, these actions are likely to be highly subjective and personalized (see **subjectivity**) and ultimately internalized by individuals as realities. These constructive processes usually stem from multiple and repetitive processes of interaction (Berger and Luckmann, 1966). In this way, it becomes possible to say that world is *socially constructed*.

For the researcher, the implication of the above argument suggests that if a constructionist approach is being followed then he or she will be studying the research **respondents'** expressions, actions and general behaviours in the research field in order to understand the sense they make. This will usually form part of espousal of an overall interpretivistic methodological approach to the research project (see **interpretivism**). In passing, it should also be noted that these research processes will involve **subjectivity** and **reflexivity** in relation to **interpreting** the **data** on the part of the researcher(s).

A second important assumption to challenge is the role of **language** in everyday life and settings which, from a social constructionist viewpoint, is not considered neutral or categorical. For many people, different words, terms or expressions may mean, signify or represent different things. Clichéd examples of this might include the oft-cited (if socially and politically problematic) thought that one person's freedom fighter is another person's terrorist.

A more everyday effect of different interpretations of language can be demonstrated by asking a group of people a seemingly simple and straightforward question and then noting the different answers that are offered. For example, ask a group of assembled people to 'Have a happy thought!' When they are subsequently asked what the thought was many answers will be offered 'my boyfriend/girlfriend', 'sitting on a warm beach', 'my family', 'my children', 'doing sport' and so on and so forth. Evidently, the language of the question produced many different interpretations of the idea of being happy. In other words, language produces different meanings and actions in different individuals and groups. In the **analysis** phase of research projects, researchers aim to interpret and understand the significance that respondents are attaching and attributing to their words and general communication. This will often involve techniques such as **constant comparison.**

Key Words
Constant Comparison, Interpretivism, Ontology, Reflexivity, Subjectivity

References
Berger and Luckmann (1966); Eriksson and Kovalainen (2008); Watson and Harris (1999)

Content Analysis

Content analysis is a process wherein communication in a given context is examined in order to determine and classify the features and characteristics that appear within it. This communication may occur in, for example, newspapers, radio, television programmes and advertisements, films, speeches, reports, pictures and so on, and is therefore essentially an **analysis** of *textual* forms (Silverman, 2010a: 243–4). The analytical process involves establishing codes that represent the characteristics in the content of the given medium under examination (Hair, Money, Samouel and Page, 2007) (see **coding**).

As a **research** technique, content analysis can take a lot of time to accomplish as each event or document has to be recorded, accessed and examined in detail. This process will usually involve drawing up a **coding** schedule, which acts as a map and glossary with which to classify and categorize each utterance, statement, expression and so on in the **data** (see Chapter 12 in Bryman and Bell, 2007).

In developing these categories, it is important to be mindful of ensuring that the categories and codings produced are clearly defined and delineated – in other words, that they do not overlap. A further factor to consider is whether or not the schedule has identified all the important codes and categories that are needed for the analysis of the content and that nothing has been overlooked.

Key Words
Analysis, Coding, Data

References
Bryman and Bell (2007); Hair, Money, Samouel and Page (2007); Silverman (2010a)

C

Context

Context means the things, events, words, issues, atmospheres – indeed the list is potentially very long – that surround, relate to, underpin and sometimes precede a given place, time and situation.

Context and its verbal form, to *contextualize,* are terms that are extensively employed in academic **discourse** and commentary. This is particularly the case in **qualitative** research. One of the reasons for this is that qualitative-style **research** attributes considerable importance to providing readers with in-depth and broad descriptions of research settings, events and people's behaviours and expression. In this way, it is felt that it will enable research to demonstrate a powerful understanding and therefore **knowledge** of the research field and the **data** generated. In other words, the assumption underlying the provision of a large amount of context in research reports, **theses** and papers is that it enables the reader to better appreciate and understand the data and findings of a given piece of research.

Key Words
Data, Qualitative

References
Silverman (2010a,b)

Control Group

A control group is a collection of people or entities that are identified for a **research** project and used to make comparisons with the *actual* research **respondents**. However, in contrast to the actual research respondents, the control group do not receive or experience the intervention or actions implemented by the **researcher.** For example, the members of the control group will not be interviewed, sent **questionnaires**, observed and so on and so forth. The purpose of this is that it allows the researcher to compare the findings from the research respondents who are subjected to these methods with a group of people who have not experienced the research project. This enables the researcher to see if effects, experiences and findings in the **data** are particular and specific to the situations and actions in the research sample and field (see **sampling**). Alternatively, it might transpire that the control group report similar data to the researched sample group. In this case, this would mean that the research sample is not especially remarkable and their experience or traits can be found more generally in a wider **population** (Maylor and Blackmon, 2005: 204–5).

Control groups do not commonly play a major role in **qualitative**, inductive or interpretative-type approaches (see **inductivism**, **interpretivism**). Typically, they are seen as an important aspect of experimental, scientific, positivistic forms of research work (see **experimental design**, **positivism**) (Bryman and Bell,

2007: 44–53). These latter types of research approach have episte-mological and ontological approaches towards establishing and identifying **truth** and **validity** that differ from other approaches (see **ontology**, **epistemology**, **interpretivism**, **positivism**). Following an experimentalist approach, it is believed that a control group assists in isolating the cause and effects between **variables** because something happens, or is identified, in the sample that does not occur in the control group (see **causality**). On the other hand, for inductive approaches, the distillation or pin-pointing of a 'truth' is not considered as being that evident or straightforward. What is seen to be 'true' is considered to be context-related, so in this regard a control group would be likely to offer different charac-teristics (that is, different contextual factors) that would make categorical comparison (in order to identify 'cause and effect' type relationships) less clear and conclusive.

Key Words
Data, Experimental Design, Population, Respondents, Sample, Truth, Validity

References
Bryman and Bell (2007); Maylor and Blackmon (2005)

Correlation

Correlation means a relationship between two things. When some-thing happens to one thing, a change or variation is likely to occur in the other. In other words, a cause and effect relationship is said to exist between them (see **causality**). In terms of **research**, correlation is the term used to gauge and assess the relationship between **variables** or two or more pieces of **data**. If the variables are said to have a *positive correlation* then, as one increases in value, the other also increases in value to some extent. If the variables are said to have a *negative correlation* then, as one variable increases, the other variable decreases in value (Ha, 2011; Payne, 2011).

Correlation is a technique drawn from within the disciplines of mathematics and **statistics**. As an approach, it is more commonly, although not exclusively, employed in deductive and positivistic types of research (see **deductivism** and **positivism**). This is prima-rily because these forms of research have philosophical commit-ments with regard to **epistemology** and **ontology** that a numerical approach espouses with regard to the notion of 'truth' and 'facts'. Indeed, in order to be able to conduct a correlation exercise the identified variables need to be **linear** and quantifiable in nature; for example, looking for a relationship between company profit levels and chief executives' salaries. Quantifiable variables are not always easily attainable. For instance, it will be very challenging to find a meaningful way of classifying, categorizing and correlating different forms of human opinion or behaviour as a variable. Although, of course, it is always possible to collect **interview** or **questionnaire** data on these issues and attempt to compare them through some means. However, this may leave a doubt over whether or not other, unidentified, unacknowledged, ambiguous or ill-defined variables or factors are in play and having influence.

Key Words
Data, Deductivism, Epistemology, Ontology, Positivism, Variable

References
Ha (2011); Payne (2011)

Covert Research

Covert means secret, disguised or hidden. Covert research is **research** which is conducted secretly without the people being researched knowing that this is the case. This clearly raises a range of ethical issues and questions (Israel and Hay, 2006) (see **ethics**). In general, covert research is very open to the charge that it is not ethical because **data** are being collected without the explicit **consent** and permission of the unknowing participants. Instances of this might particularly be found, for example, in **participant observation** approaches. An illustration of this could be social research involving observation of shopping habits in a supermarket. The researcher is able to conduct the research without shoppers knowing that they are being observed.

If covert research is considered necessary for a research project, then it will be essential that the proposed research project receives approval by the university, or other relevant internal or external ethics panels or committees.

Key Words
Consent, Ethics, Permission

References
Israel and Hay (2006)

Critical Incident Method (CIM)

Critical incident method (CIM) is a **research** technique that aims to collect and analyse **data** by identifying particular moments or situations that exemplify or illustrate a particular issue or topic. This can be achieved by asking research respondents questions that invite them to think about events that have occurred and reveal or underline particular points. For example, the research project might be about various kinds of bullying in the workplace and the **researcher** might ask if the **respondent** can think of any occasion when they felt bullied through email. Evidently, CIM often takes place through **interviews** and will involve questions like: 'What led up to the event?', 'Who did and said what to whom?', 'What happened next?' 'What were you thinking and feeling at that moment?' and 'What was the outcome?' (paraphrased from Bryman and Bell, 2007: 228).

Of course, a precondition for the suitability of CIM is that it must be possible in the situation and **context** under examination to anticipate that respondents will *be able to* identify critical incidents. The **concept** of 'critical incidents', in its wider sense, has been particularly employed for a number of years in attempts to analyse a range of public service contexts including, for example, education and health care (Ghaye and Lillyman, 2008; Tripp, 1993).

Key Words
Concept, Context, Incident, Situation

References
Bryman and Bell (2007); Ghaye and Lillyman (2008); Tripp (1993)

C

Critical Management Studies (CMS)

CMS is a particular set of approaches to organization and management that has emerged and developed over the past two to three decades. The advent of CMS has led to a wide range of papers and texts typically adopting inductive and interpretive methodologies (see **inductivism**, **interpretivism** and **research methodology**). **Critical Theory**, in particular, had an influential role at the beginnings of the movement (see Alvesson and Willmott, 1992, 1996).

CMS commentaries have engaged a wide variety of methodological stances and approaches including, among others, existentialism, **postmodernism**, **poststructuralism**, **critical realism** and **deconstructionism**. It is uncommon, indeed rare, for CMS approaches to employ positivistic-type methodologies (see **positivism**).

There are a number of CMS-influenced conferences such as the Standing Conference on Organizational Symbolism (SCOS); European Group on Organizational Studies (EGOS) and the bi-annual International Critical Management Studies Conference (CMS). Moreover, there are a number of journals that tend to publish CMS-style publications (for example *Organization; Organization Studies; Culture and Organization; Ephemera*).

Key Words
Critical Realism, Deconstructionism, Positivism, Postmodernism, Poststructuralism, Reflexivity, Subjectivity

References
Alvesson and Willmott (1992, 1996); Clegg, Kornberger and Pitsis (2011); Linstead, Fulop and Lilley (2009)

Critical Realism

Critical realism is a philosophical and methodological approach that assumes that, through use of the human senses, what people initially perceive can be said to constitute a statement of being true and accurate. As such, this offers some *notion* of objective perception or observation (see **objectivity**). However, subsequent closer examination of a given object or phenomenon may well produce a range of reactions and *interpretations* and hence also invoke subjective aspects into the way something might be understood (see **subjectivity**).

Therefore, it can be seen that critical realism emphasizes the notion of 'what is' and ideas of solid reality, that is, **ontology**, and the way it shapes our perceptions to a greater degree than more relativistic approaches such as, for example, **postmodernism** and **poststructuralism** (see **relativism**).

Bhaskar (1989) is generally considered to be a seminal early commentator on critical realism; however, it has been widely adopted and employed, often based on ethnographic and interpretive approaches in a range of disciplinary domains including organization and management **research** (see illustrations and elaborations in

Ackroyd and Fleetwood, 2001; Contu and Willmott, 2005; Fairclough, 2005; Fleetwood, 2005; Fleetwood and Ackroyd, 2004; Reed, 2005; Willmott, 2005) (see **ethnography** and **interpretivism**).

Key Words
Ethnography, Interpretivism, Objectivity, Ontology, Positivism, Postmodernism, Poststructuralism, Subjectivity

References
Ackroyd and Fleetwood (2001); Bhaskar (1989); Contu and Willmott (2005); Fairclough (2005); Fleetwood (2005); Fleetwood and Ackroyd (2004); Mutch (2005); Reed (2005); Willmott (2005)

Critical Theory

Critical Theory is a philosophy that emerged from the Frankfurt School, which was based around the Institute of Social Research in Frankfurt during the 1920s and 1930s but conducted **research** also in the post-war period. Critical Theory is associated with names such as Marcuse (1898–1979), Horkheimer (1895–1973), Adorno (1903–1969), Fromm (1900–1980) and Habermas (1929–). Critical Theory has proved to be a very influential philosophy in the social sciences including organiz-ation and management studies. Its ideology is particularly concerned with the pursuit of emancipation for people and society from the alienating effects of **modernism** and has the ambition of creating a more integrated and comprehensive societal response.

In methodological terms, adoption of a critical theoretical approach embodies an attempt to seek to understand issues such as alienation, emancipation, **identity**, **meaning**, power, resistance, change and transformation in human situations. It is most likely to involve **research methods** that facilitate the collection of rich infor-mation and may well make use of a range of **qualitative** and **quan-titative data.** Typical research methods used within such an approach would be, by way of illustration, semi-structured or unstruc-tured **interviews**, **participant observation** or **focus groups**.

Key Words
Alienation, Emancipation, Frankfurt School

References
Alvesson and Willmott (1992, 1996); Malpas and Wake (2006); Sim and Van Loon (2005)

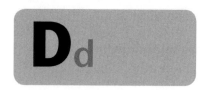

Dd

Data

Data are known facts, items, details and so on and so forth regarding certain contexts or **research** settings in relation to which inference and understanding can be drawn. Data is a plural term and therefore will be written as, for example: 'the data *are* ...' (rather than 'the data *is* ...' which, in formal research settings, is incorrect). Data are commonly at the heart of any piece of research.

There a number of adjectives that can be attached to 'data'. A major categorization is the use of the terms *primary data* and *secondary data*. **Primary data** are data that have been collected at source usually by the **researcher(s),** or associates undertaking the research in question. This is new and fresh data that have been collected for the specific research in hand. The research team will have designed the research study and planned which data, and from which sources, are appropriate and necessary to collect.

On the other hand, **secondary data** are data that have already been collected and assembled for a purpose other than the current project. This could include items such as books, **statistics** and documents. Although it is not usually the case, it is possible these data may also have been collected at an earlier point in time for a previous project.

Discrete data are data that can be easily separated out and counted. This might not always be possible such as with observations or **interview** conversations.

Processes and **methods** within a piece of research or research project concerning data are likely to include: **data collection**, data **analysis**, data **triangulation** and data presentation.

Key Words
Analysis, Data Collection, Discrete Data, Primary Data, Secondary Data

References
Bryman and Bell (2007)

Data Collection

Data collection involves the many different ways in which **data** for a specific piece of **research** are gathered and organized. The data collection is determined by the **aims** and the **objectives** of the study and the overall design of the study in response to these. It should be noted that data collection is a key standard phase of most research work and projects (Silverman, 2010a,b).

In terms of the act of data collection, this is accomplished through a wide range of available **research methods** that have the purpose of gathering **quantitative** and **qualitative** data. These methods might typically include **interviews**, **focus groups** and **questionnaires** and so on and so forth. Each of these methods is likely to use varying forms of questions in order to secure the appropriate data.

In addition, the data collection stage(s) of a research project will have been preceded by a **research design** that plans **access** to the data and ensures that guidelines on **ethics** have been adhered to.

Key Words
Aim, Data, Ethics, Interview, Focus Group, Objective, Quantitative, Qualitative, Questionnaire, Research Method

References
Silverman (2010a,b)

Deconstructionism

Deconstructionism is a philosophy elaborated primarily by the French philosopher Jacques Derrida (1930–2004). It is often associated with **postmodernism** and **poststructuralism.** Deconstructionism is seen as concerned with **textual analysis** and in particular identifying deeply embedded structures, or oppositions, in texts (see Derrida 1973, 1976). A deconstructive process challenges the notion of any 'inherent' **meaning** in a given text. Derrida advocated that a particular text is not finalized or 'fixed' in meaning, alternatively suggesting that meaning is ephemeral and derived from the historical origins and contemporary context in which text is set. Jones (2004) has noted that deconstructionism is often perceived in a negative way. This may be in part because of its very label, which can give a sense of destruction, but equally it may be connected to the controversy that Derrida attracted throughout his life.

D

It is not that common to see an overt deconstructive approach in use in a document like a **dissertation** or a **thesis**. Nevertheless, deconstructionism has played, and continues to play, a role in the **research** published in journal articles. This tends to comprise work being carried out under the umbrella of certain branches of **critical management studies**.

The use of deconstructionism in research is most likely to lead to some form of approach that employs **hermeneutic** or **discourse analysis**. Typically, this would involve the **researcher** gathering interpretive, **qualitative** style **data**, through, for example, **interviews**, **participant observation**, or the study of various forms and sources of text. It is important to remember that the term *text* covers not only something that is written or spoken but also a wide range of other potential forms including non-verbal (for example body **language**, sound other than voice).

Key Words

Discourse, Hermeneutics, Meaning, Postmodernism, Poststructuralism

References

Chia (1996); Cooper (1989); Derrida (1973, 1976); Jones (2004, 2007, 2010)

Deductivism

Deductivism is a philosophical approach that can be used in conducting **research**. Within deductivism, the theoretical framework, questions and **hypotheses** of a piece of research are first developed and then subsequently applied to **data** that have been collected in the field (see **data collection**) (Cameron and Price, 2009: 74–8).

In other words, the process of deductivism develops the main aspects of its theoretical framework at the initial stages of the research project. This general, or overall, schema is then used to comment on individual, specific or particular cases and instances in order to make decisions determining to what extent the specific case fits with that framework or not.

The deductive approach is generally associated with positivistic and experimentationalist-style methodologies (see **positivism** and **experimental design**). Deductivism shares with these approaches a valuing of the idea of **objectivity** and a predilection to use **quantitative** measures.

Deductivism differs and contrasts with inductivist approaches (see **inductivism**).

Key Words
Data, Experimental Design, Objectivity, Positivism

References
Cameron and Price (2009)

Delphi Technique

The Delphi technique is a **research method** for obtaining **data** and **information** by using expert panels. It is particularly useful as a means of predicting the evolution and development of future events based on informed insight and opinion.

The early stages of Delphi technique generally involve identifying a series of issues or possible scenarios that are central and relevant to the desired questions and themes of the **research**. The next phase usually involves the **researchers** drawing up **questionnaires** which are sent out to a number of commentators and experts carefully identified as opinion influencers or leaders in the field. It is usually the case that the various **respondents** are not in contact with, or are not even directly aware of, each other as participants in the research. They complete and return the questionnaire and the results are summarized and fed back anonymously to the original respondents. The **objective** is for the contributors to achieve some convergence of viewpoint and indication of likely future trends (Fisher, 2010: 160). As variations of this process, it is also possible to have the group of people in the same room and, after the initial briefing on research, to also allow them to seek clarification on the themes.

D

Delphi technique: mini-case illustration

The researchers wanted to investigate the implementation of a healthy eating and well-being policy in schools in a particular region. They were conducting this research from a public health discipline organizational perspective.

In order to ensure that the research would take account of extant thinking on the subject, the researchers designed a two-stage study. The first stage consisted of a Delphi technique approach used with identified and well-respected key academics, public health directors, government officials and so on and so forth.

This allowed the researchers to generate a series of key, prevalent and recurring themes and issues in the field.

In the second phase, from these themes, the researchers compiled a questionnaire that would explore and investigate the themes further. This questionnaire was sent out to over a hundred identified co-ordinators responsible for promoting and overseeing healthy schools policy. This, in turn, was followed up by one–one recorded and transcribed interviews with certain co-ordinators. This second phase of the research generated a series of codes or terms within earlier generated themes. The codes were used to analyse and codify the transcripts from the respondents.

Key Words
Questionnaire, Respondents, Scenario

References
Fisher (2010)

Determinism

Determinism is the belief in the notion of cause and effect existing between entities and events (see **causality**). The word determinism comes from the fact that one event or issue is *determined* by an event or issue that precedes it. It is central to a scientific approach to **research** and important feature of **research methodologies** that are based on **positivism**. In line with its scientific and positivistic alignment, the **concepts** of **objectivity** and **rationalism** are very important (see **positivism**). In contrast, **subjectivity** is not seen as playing a role in the **data** and in all cases attempts are likely to be made in order to remove what is seen as **bias**.

For some social scientists, determinism is seen to represent a sometimes oversimplified version of action, interaction and consequence (see Bryman and Bell, 2007: 627). Rather than one event being directly caused by another, they are more likely to question the very **identity** and boundaries of such 'events' and 'issues' and may be persuaded to try to make sense of data and situations through an alternative emergent, social constructionist, postmodern or post-structural manner (see **sense-making, postmodernism, post-structuralism, social constructionism**).

Key Words
Bias, Objectivity, Positivism, Rationalism, Subjectivity

References
Bryman and Bell (2007); Erola (2010)

Discourse (Analysis)

Discourse involves transaction, exchange and communication through all means and forms including, by way of example, voice, text and sound. Discourse is often the focus of interest and study in the social sciences. The investigation of discourse – its patterns, structures and meanings – is commonly encompassed in a **research method** and methodological approach called 'discourse analysis'. Discussions on discourse are likely to involve terms such as **language**, signs, narratives, storytelling or symbols (see **narrative research** and **semiotics**). Where embedded and repeated patterns of discourse are identified in **data** and observations, they are often referred to as *discursive practice(s)* (Grant, Hardy, Oswick and Putnam, 2004; Phillips, Sewell and Jaynes, 2008).

In terms of **research methodology**, discourse analysis, is a relatively common approach within inductive, interpretivistic and **qualitative** approaches (see **inductivism** and **interpretivism**). Typically, these approaches involve the use of methods and techniques to deconstruct and illustrate (although not always in the sense of **deconstructionism** and its methodological principles) the subjective processes taking place in the discourse(s) under examination (Fairclough, 2010) (see **subjectivity**). **Researchers** employing discourse analysis are often particularly interested in identifying and illustrating issues of power, **identity** and **meaning** and how these are subjectively produced and reproduced in various settings.

Key Words
Inductivism, Interpretivism, Language, Meaning, Objectivity, Ontology, Positivism, Storytelling, Subjectivity

D

References
Fairclough (2010); Grant, Hardy, Oswick and Putnam (2004); Phillips, Sewell and Jaynes (2008)

Discrete Data (*see* Data)

Discussion

A discussion is the process of talking or relating ideas and information in a systematic and reasoned manner. In other words, it is about conveying ideas in a logical and coherent way. In a generic sense, discussion and the ability to conduct discussion are an integral element of any piece of **research** writing.

In a more specific, technical sense, 'the discussion' of a research project or paper refers to a particular section of a document or paper. The 'discussion' section normally follows, or is linked into, the findings of a project. It is at this point that the preceding **introduction**, **literature review**, **research methodology** section and findings are drawn together in an attempt to elaborate and begin to address and respond to the research **aims**, **objectives** and questions in a concerted and meaningful manner (Thody, 2006).

It is imperative that a discussion contains extensive critical **analysis** of the materials it is considering. This means that the literature and collected **data** need to be scrutinized and weighed up in relation to the questions the research is trying to answer. For the writer, this will involve challenging and questioning whether he or she agrees with how the literature relates to the questions and data and vice versa.

Key Words
Aims, Literature Review, Objectives, Research Methodology

References
Thody (2006)

Dissertation

D

A dissertation is an integral piece of **research** that usually forms a final part of the work for an undergraduate or taught postgraduate academic course of study. As such, it is written in an academic rather than a practitioner style. In terms of structure, dissertations are usually composed of the following typical sections:

- *Introduction*
- *Research Aims and Objectives*
- *Literature Review*
- *Research Methodology*

- *Findings*
- **Discussion**
- *Conclusion*
- *Bibliography*
- *Appendices (if required)*

These sections may vary to some extent depending on particular requirements of projects and institutions. The length of a dissertation will also vary but for undergraduate level work it will normally range between 10,000 and 12,000 words and for postgraduate programmes it will situate in the order of 18,000 to 20,000 words in length (Biggam, 2008; Greetham, 2009).

Many students approach the time of doing a dissertation with some anxiety and concern. To some extent, this can be addressed by starting the process early and working in a regular way on each section. This might be alternatively phrased as the idea of approaching large tasks in a 'chunk and chip' way. In other words, try to avoid seeing the dissertation as an almost impossible mountain to be climb, rather, break what needs to be done into bits, sections or 'chunks' that are very manageable in a relatively short space of time. This can then be tackled relatively easily or 'chipped away at' bit by bit.

Key Words
Discussion, Literature Review, Research Methodology

References
Biggam (2008); Greetham (2009)

Distribution

D

Distribution is a technical term used in **research methodology** to indicate the pattern or the manner in which **data** occurrences are spread out, or distributed, among the sample (see **sampling**).

Key Words
Data, Population, Sampling

References
Saunders, Lewis and Thornhill (2007)

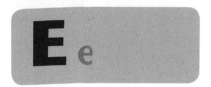

Emic

Emic is a term used to refer to an account or story that is created by the participants or **respondents** providing an account for the **research** (see **narrative research**). In this way it is a representation of the research that is produced 'internally' by participants using their own **language** and **discourse**, from within the research setting or field (see Ailon, 2006; Eriksson and Kovalainen, 2008; Wolfram Cox and Hassard, 2005). In general terms, emic contexts are very bound up with the specific cultures where they are set or situated.

Emic accounts contrast with **etic** accounts which tend to be produced by external agents such as **researchers**.

Key Words
Discourse, Respondents, Storytelling

References
Ailon (2006); Eriksson and Kovalainen (2008); Wolfram Cox and Hassard (2005)

Empiricism

In methodological terms, empiricism means that **data** and **knowledge** are built up through **researchers** employing the human senses and taking observations on a tentative prima facie observational or face-value basis (see **epistemology**). This may seem a self-evident thing to say with regard to any methodological approach; however, some approaches, such as **experimental design**, see a purely empirical approach as being prone to allowing **subjectivity** to enter the **research** process, **data** and findings rather than maintaining **objectivity** (see also **positivism**). Empiricism is commonly seen as a historically central value and approach in Anglo-Saxon contexts.

Key Words
Anglo-Saxon, Epistemology, Human Senses, Meaning, Positivism, Sense-making, Scientific Experimentation

References
Bryman and Bell (2007); Tadajewski (2009); Whitley (2003)

Epistemology

Epistemology is derived from the Greek word *episteme*, which means **knowledge** (that is, the act of knowing, awareness and securing information). Epistemology is therefore concerned with theories about how and why knowledge is made and, as such, it constitutes an important branch of philosophy. Knowledge and the processes and principles in operation when generating **data** and knowledge are, of course, central concerns of **research** and **research methodologies.** When the term *epistemology* is employed in research methodology contexts, it points at the assumptions a **researcher** uses as he or she goes about generating data and creating knowledge**.** It is, therefore, vital for students engaged in research projects to develop a clear understanding of what is involved in this term and how it impacts on their work.

Epistemology – Questions on which to reflect …

In practical terms for your methodology, there are a number of broad issues and questions that can help in identifying epistemological assumptions which may be in operation. These are useful to keep in mind when developing the methodology for a research project:

1 What is the conventionally or commonly stated position of your chosen methodological approach in terms of the role of **subjectivity** or **objectivity** in the process of creation of knowledge through that methodology? In other words, do you believe that, by using that approach, you are developing data that will be objective or do you believe that some subjectivities will have *legitimately* played a role in the emergence of the data?

2 And, linked to this, what is the position of your chosen methodological approach in terms of whether the knowledge created has an existence *external* (that is, leaning towards trying to be objective) to the researcher? Or, alternatively, is the researcher *implicated and involved* (that is, subjectivities are acknowledged as playing a role) in the knowledge creation?

3 What are the position and characteristics of your chosen approach in terms of **inductivism** (knowledge being derived from data in an emergent and **iterative** way that acknowledges the role of subjectivity) or **deductivism** (building knowledge by developing and testing **hypotheses** in as objective a way as possible)?

E

Understanding the epistemological stance of a piece of research is not a process that students have to undertake necessarily from first principles. Over the centuries, debates on philosophy and methodology have generated a wide range of established differing epistemological positions and schools of thought, for example **positivism**, **interpretivism** and **postmodernism** to name but a few. It is possible to think of the epistemological positions of these approaches as being composed of a series of traditions, each having its own history, political stance and commitments.

Any piece of research work needs to adopt, develop and be seen to adhere to its identified and chosen epistemological stance. In other words, when you choose or develop a methodology for your work, you must make clear and reinforce the epistemological assumptions of your espoused methodology. Equally, if you expressly choose a given methodological and epistemological approach, it automatically invokes and points at the assumptions you make and the thoughts you have regarding what is the most appropriate or preferred way of inquiring or examining a research subject or area. It shows the informed reader about how you view the world and how you think it should, perhaps, be usefully seen by others. It is an integral part of the argument you are making in the research.

Above all, an awareness of the existence and the role of epistemology reminds us that we should not accept as a given, or take for granted, the processes of knowledge formation. We must always ask questions about how, why and when particular knowledge came into being and came to be accepted as valid. By understanding the assumptions and roots of knowledge formation, we are ultimately able to challenge, test and question the **validity** and authenticity of that knowledge according to the principles it adheres to.

E

Summary key points on epistemology for your research work:

- Remember that 'knowledge is made' and that, as part of your research, *you chose the process for making knowledge* – the pre-existence of any knowledge is not a given.
- Remember that there *already exists a range of long-established research methodological and philosophical approaches (for example positivism, interpretivism and so on)* each with its own epistemological stance and commitments – read about your chosen approach and become aware of the assumptions that underpin it.
- In conducting all the stages of your research, **literature review**, methodology, findings, **discussion** and **analysis** and **writing up**, keep in mind that the epistemological stance of your chosen methodology should run coherently throughout the entire work.

Key Words
Analysis, Assumptions, Knowledge, Methodology, Researcher

References
Bryman and Bell (2007); Denzin and Lincoln (2008); Eriksson and Kovalainen (2008)

Ethics

Ethics is an aspect of philosophy that is concerned with choices and decisions about what is right and wrong and good and bad. Clearly, in some regards this will be a subjective process and outcome. What is considered 'good' from one viewpoint may seem very 'bad' from another stance.

Outside of methodological considerations, ethics constitutes a significant field with a large collection of writings. With regard to the application of ethical considerations to **research methods**, this has, in recent decades, become of increasing interest and generated a wide range of commentary. In broad terms, the ethical considerations within a piece of **research** aim to ensure that no harm, or 'bad' is experienced by the **researcher** or the **respondents** before, during or after the conduct of the research project.

In many domains and institutions, it is common to have an ethics committee which verifies and endorses studies (or not) before they are allowed to take place. This, of course, does not remove or abrogate the role of the researcher to take full responsibility for all actions and plans in relation to the given research. Equally, many professional associations and bodies have produced guidelines or advice notes in relation to ethics in research and these are well worth consulting before designing and commencing a study.

> *Bulmer (2008) provides a number of useful core considerations that should be taken into account when undertaking research:*
>
> - The issues of ensuring and safeguarding **confidentiality** and **anonymity** of **data** and **respondents**
> - The importance of securing informed **consent** in research
> - The serious step of deceit and lying in the course of research
> - Use, and justification, of **covert** observation
> - Consideration of what is permissible to ask in **surveys**, **interviews** and **questionnaires**
> - Respect for privacy
> - Attending to the consequences of publication
>
> (Paraphrased from Bulmer, 2008)

E

Exploring a number of these points in greater depth, as part of an ethical research approach, it is considered important to seek the informed **consent** of the participants before commencing the research. In this way, people are aware when the research will be taking place (if they have agreed to it) and of what it consists. A further ethical consideration is the matter of whether or not there are any vested interests active in the research. An example here might include sponsorship of the research project. This should be declared when the research is being undertaken and to not do so may cause tensions and difficulties at a later date when it comes to light.

Key Words
Anonymity, Confidentiality, Deceit, Informed Consent, Privacy

References
Jones, Parker, Ten Bos (2005); Israel and Hay (2006); Oliver (2010); Wray-Bliss (2002, 2004); Wray-Bliss and Brewis (2008).

Ethnography

Ethnography is a term derived from the Greek word *ethnos* meaning 'nation'. It is a **research** methodological approach that involves the study of groups and communities of people and how they live and create sense and meaning of their cultures, setting(s) and environment(s). Ethnography places great importance on studying human interactions in their *naturalistic environment* (rather than, for example, in a scientific laboratory or groups created artificially for the purposes of the research). This will involve the **researcher** spending substantial time in the place where people live and work, for example with an office team, a factory workforce, a street community, a jungle tribe, a school, a classroom and so on and so forth. For this reason, ethnographic types of research frequently employ methods such as **participant observation** and unstructured **interviews**. These methods are often considered less intrusive and disruptive than alternatives, such as a **questionnaire** or structured interview. These latter approaches need to be formally set up and conducted and thereby are prone to interrupting the 'natural' flow of behaviour and activity.

Ethnography can be employed in a range of studies although it predominantly forms part of a **qualitative** approach. Ethnography

E

will almost inevitably involve acknowledgement of the role of **subjectivity** in creation of the research **data**. Different research will of course express a wide span of comments and opinions on what appear to be similar 'facts'. The application of ethnographic techniques to the data is believed to allow a richer portrayal of emotional and **lived experience** aspects of the field. Due to this, ethnography is commonly used in, for example, **critical management studies.**

It is useful to note that a number of worthwhile and valuable conferences take place in relation to ethnographic methodological approaches. One such example is the annual conference run by the Management School at Liverpool University in the UK, often in collaboration with partner institutions.

Key Words
Emotion, Lived Experience, Mainstream, Naturalistic, Participant Observation, Research Methodology, Sense-making, Subjectivity

References
Alvesson and Deetz (2000); Alvesson and Sköldberg (2009); Bryman and Bell (2007); Humphreys, Brown and Hatch (2003); Van Maanen (1988)

Etic

Etic is a term that refers to an account that is produced from the outside, or externally from a given **research** setting. It is an account produced by, for example, a **researcher** examining a given research domain. In doing this, the researcher is likely to be approaching the field with a particular **frame of reference** or theoretical framework. This may well predetermine or shape the manner in which **data** are collected and analysed and the **language** and **discourse** employed to facilitate this. In this overall sense, etic conveys the idea of some sense of detachment from the specific culture being examined.

Emic differs from etic in that an emic account is one produced internally by research participants and **respondents** and therefore the data are likely to be shaped or framed in a manner that makes direct sense to them rather than being structured for the convenience of the research project (Ailon, 2006; Eriksson and Kovalainen, 2008; Wolfram Cox and Hassard, 2005).

E

Key Words
Data, Frame of Reference, Respondent

References
Ailon (2006); Eriksson and Kovalainen (2008); Wolfram Cox and Hassard (2005)

Evaluation

Evaluation concerns processes of appraising and judging **data, research methods** and literature (see **literature review**) to see if they are, in the first instance, appropriate for using in, and progressing, a given **research** project. There are a range of various questions and issues that need to be considered in relation to evaluating different research methods (see Eriksson and Kovalainen, 2008). Moreover, there are issues relating to **validity**, **reliability** and **generalizability** of the research data and findings (Gill and Johnson, 2010).

Key Words
Data, Generalizability, Reliability, Research Methods, Validity

References
Eriksson and Kovalainen (2008); Gill and Johnson (2010)

Experimental Design

Experimental design is a type of **research methodology**. The pattern or process of this approach typically includes the following stages:

- Development of a **hypothesis** or hypotheses
- (leading on from the above stage) Identify the **variables** (dependent and independent) that will allow the hypothesis to be tested, proven or disproved
- Put the experiment into effect and check for the presence of any additional factors (or extraneous variables) that may have produced changes other than the identified and measured variables

An example of this might be, for instance, an attempt to measure the impact of wage increases on productivity levels of workers. This

E

would aim to see if an increase in wages leads to an increase in productivity (see also Dahl, Mo and Vannucci, 2008; Meade, Michels and Lautenschlager, 2007).

Like all methodologies, experimental design comes with a number of underlying methodological and philosophical assumptions:

- It aims to be objective and to secure **objectivity** around its design, **data collection** and findings. This means that these aspects must not be 'contaminated' or affected by subjectivities of the **researcher.**
- In establishing hypotheses, it assumes that there is a pre-established or already existing truth 'out there' in the **research** setting and world that can be identified, located, isolated and proved or disproved.
- Through the development of variables, which are clearly defined and delineated from the rest of the world, experimental design underlines that it has a realist ontological perspective (see **realism** and **ontology**). Experimental design sees the relationship between these variables as deterministic, meaning that direct 'cause and effect' interactions take place between them (see **determinism**). This contrasts with, for example, interpretivistic styles of study, which generally consider that a multiplicity of factors and issues are likely to be interacting and influencing a research environment at any given period (see **interpretivism**).
- By establishing hypotheses, it tends to start by stating broad propositions regarding how the world 'is' or 'is not'. From this general position, it moves on to analyse and identify more specific positions and cases. This is a process known as **deductivism**.
- It generally approaches aspects of research environments such as, for example, **language**, **discourse** and power, as fixed and given. This often differs from other approaches such as **inductivism** (Maylor and Blackmon, 2005: 200–10).

E

Key Words
Deductivism, Determinism, Epistemology, Hypothesis, Inductivism, Objectivity, Ontology, Variable

References
Dahl, Mo and Vannucci (2008); Maylor and Blackmon (2005); Meade, Michels and Lautenschlager (2007)

Focus Group

A focus group is a **research method** that involves the **researcher(s)** organizing a collection of **research** participants or **respondents** into a group with the **aim** of discussing and collating views on a particular topic or issue. Focus groups are supplied with the topic to be considered by the researcher. A key aspect of focus groups is that participants speak about the allocated item or topic from their own personal experiences (Eriksson and Kovalainen, 2008). Focus groups can be employed as the unique method in a research project but quite often they may be used in conjunction with another method such as **interviews**, **questionnaires** or **participant observation**.

Focus groups are used across a wide range of areas including, for example, to gain views and opinions on government policy, political parties, commercial advertising campaigns, new product development – the potential list is endless. Focus groups are excellent for gaining rich and in-depth attitudes and opinions on issues. Equally, however, it should be remembered that, just like in any other social gathering, some individuals may dominate and 'hog' airtime and this may need to be managed or facilitated to some extent by the researcher.

There are a number of challenges for the researcher with using focus groups. Firstly, because the conversation is free and open between participants, it can sometimes be difficult to record or follow. In other words, like any other conversation, there are points when everyone can sometimes seem to be talking at once! Secondly, co-ordinating people to attend focus groups can be very difficult with participants cancelling and or simply not turning up. This can mean that the progress of a project's research strategy can be hindered. Many of these potential difficulties can be overcome if time is put into planning the topics, the necessary and desired composition of the groups, the timings and location of the sessions and the recruitment process used to secure participants (Farnsworth and Boon, 2010; Halkier, 2010).

Key Words
Attitudes, Opinions, Respondents

References
Eriksson and Kovalainen (2008); Farnsworth and Boon (2010); Halkier (2010).

Frame of Reference

When we employ the term *frame of reference* we are often thinking of, and referring to, the general manner in which a particular person or group have come to view an issue or range of **contexts**. This view will be based on the assumptions, presuppositions and points of view that they have developed through processes of socialization or education over a period of time (see **social constructionism**). Equally, it may constitute an adopted set of values for a particular context or project. Additionally, the way a person perceives approaches and consequently addresses an environment inevitably has effects in, and for, that setting. In essence, therefore, we can see a frame of reference as a collection of accumulated and reinforced beliefs, principles and boundaries that people hold and that guide their actions. Of course, these are more than likely to be a wide range of different frames of reference held by different individuals.

In more technical **language**, we can also say that a person's frame of reference embodies the epistemological and ontological assumptions and beliefs regarding the world and what exists and occurs therein (see **epistemology** and **ontology**). Equally, in trying to encapsulate the way a person generally makes sense of issues it may, on occasion, be pertinent to use the term *Gestalt* (pointing at the **concept** of 'wholeness' – see illustrative use of the term in Johnsen and Gudmand-Høyer, 2010; Martens, 2006) or **Weltanschauung** (meaning 'world view') (Bell and Taylor, 2004; Tadajewski, 2009). Furthermore, in the natural sciences (for example physics and chemistry), the term *frame of reference* specifically indicates a set of co-ordinates or plots which locate and measure the situation and position of an object. It can be seen that there is a comparable meaning to the social sciences in which it points to where people see something as being situated or coming from.

F

Key Words
Epistemology, Gestalt, Ontology, Viewpoint, Weltanschauung

References
Bell and Taylor (2004); Johnsen and Gudmand-Høyer (2010); Martens (2006); Tadajewski (2009)

Frequency

A frequency indicates the number of times a given **variable** (being examined as part of a piece of **research**) occurs. In other words, how many times did 'X' take place or how many of 'X' are there. These frequencies may often be presented in a *frequency table* that lists the various categories, items or variables for which **data** are being collected and presents the frequencies, numbers or counts of each item alongside them (Jehn, 1993, 2010; Lam, Green and Bordignon, 2002).

Key Words
Frequency Table, Variable

References
Jehn (1993, 2010); Lam, Green and Bordignon (2002)

Functionalism

Functionalism is a philosophy that is based on seeing events and structures in terms of the functions (or purposes or operations) they are intended to carry out. Functionalism tends to categorize *functions* by employing boundaries and delineations. For this reason, it can be considered by some commentators as a reductionist approach in that it attempts to simplify complex situations and phenomena (see **reductionism**). A functionalist perspective is therefore grounded in rationalistic views of **research** and it is likely that deductivist and positivistic approaches tend to be employed alongside it (see **rationalism**, **deductivism** and **positivism**) (for illustrations of issues surrounding functionalism, see Brar, 2003; Donaldson, 2005; Kirkpatrick and Ackroyd, 2003; Perrow, 2008).

Key Words
Deductivism, Positivism, Reductionist

References
Brar (2003); Donaldson (2005); Kirkpatrick and Ackroyd (2003); Perrow (2008)

F

Generalizability

Generalizability concerns the extent to which the findings of the **research** that has been conducted are relevant in another setting or situation. This is important because it helps us to understand the degree to which we can use, and get further value from, a given piece of research. Generalizability, together with **validity** and **reliability**, constitutes a test to which all research needs to be subjected.

Due to their differing approaches to **epistemology** and **ontology**, as a general rule, with inductivist interpretivistic approaches it tends to be more difficult to generalize widely than, say, with deductivist positivistic approaches (see **inductivism, interpretivism, deductivism** and **positivism**). This is because **interpretive research** tends to use small, localized samples (for example **data** developed from a limited number of **interviews** or **case studies**) and seek to illustrate that particular local situation. While this type of research recognizes that there may be similarities and commonalities between this research setting and other broadly comparable places, it also acknowledges that other settings are likely to present their own nuances and idiosyncrasies. This is in large part because inductive approaches do not espouse the idea of 'the one truth' applicable to a wide range of people and situations being readily 'findable out there'. These approaches are much more likely to see some form of **social constructionism** and **subjectivity** at play in the **sense-making** in each and every possible research setting.

Conversely, studies embracing **deductivism** and **positivism** are prepared to identify 'truths' that can stand across a broad sample. In pursuit of this goal, these forms of research will generally involve large samples that **aim** to represent the **population** of a given domain. It is also possible that some form of numerical or statistical method will be used and that a notion of **objectivity** will be envisaged for the research (see Hultsch, MacDonald, Hunter, Maitland and Dixon, 2002).

Quinton and Smallbone (2006) remind us of the work of Paul Raimond (1993) where he examined classic studies in business management and organization including Peters and Waterman's text on 'excellence' and Hofstede's work on the interface of national and corporate cultures. He provides a very useful and competent **analysis** showing how a range of issues surrounding generalizability (in conjunction with **reliability** and **validity**) are present in these works.

Key Words
Deductivism, Epistemology, Inductivism, Interpretivism, Objectivity, Ontology, Positivism, Sense-making, Social Constructionism, Subjectivity

References
Hultsch, MacDonald, Hunter, Maitland and Dixon (2002); Quinton and Smallbone (2006); Raimond (1993)

Grounded Theory

Grounded Theory is a particular methodological approach. In its early history, and subsequently, it is closely associated with a number of particular authors, including Glaser and Strauss (1967), Strauss and Corbin (1998) and subsequently Charmaz (2006) and Goulding (2002).

Grounded Theory is an inductive methodological approach (see **inductivism**). In practical terms, conducting Grounded Theory within a piece of **research** involves making the initial decision to examine a particular domain in connection with a set of issues or questions. Then, **data collection** takes place, typically using methods such as recorded **interviews** in the field or at the research site. When a body of **data** has been collected these data are subjected to progressive processes of **coding** – namely, *open coding, axial coding* and *selective coding*. In simple, everyday terms, the general idea here is to start with big clusters or themes (produced through open-coding processes) that are apparent or emerge in the data. Then the next phase (of axial coding) aims to identify subdivisions or subcategories within the broader themes established in the first phase. The data are then reread and combed again to see how they fit into the thus far constructed framework (selective coding). Through this process the broader and overall **theory** is gradually built up and emerges.

Because Grounded Theory is based on inductive and interpretivistic characteristics and commitments, this means that the emergence of the themes and related theoretical frameworks is an **iterative** and emergent process that acknowledges that **subjectivity** will be involved (see **interpretivism**). It is largely through processes of **constant comparison** with the original data, with **respondents** and with independent verifiers that the themes and categories within inductive-style research are created and crystallized.

It is important to make a cautionary note in connection with Grounded Theory. Since its inception, Grounded Theory has been widely used in research and critiqued and commented in literature. This extensive adoption is to be commended and its replete success should not be underplayed. However, like many situations where populist and commonplace usage occurs, this has not always done a great service to the name of Grounded Theory. It is not uncommon to hear a student or paper author state that they are using Grounded Theory when in fact they are not. Rather than following the highly systematic coding approach of Grounded Theory, these acts of partial adoption are, in fact, effectively just inductive and interpretive in nature. This is of course completely fine but it is important not to state that it is Grounded Theory that is being used. Overall, Grounded Theory has been employed to produce a wide range of research. Nevertheless, some commentators (of inductive and deductive persuasion alike) find it cumbersome, contrived, over-structured and artificial and, ultimately, a misleading approach in relation to the work involved and the messages the data might supply.

Key Words
Coding, Constant Comparison, Data, Inductive, Interpretivism, Subjectivity

References
Charmaz (2006); Glaser and Strauss (1967); Goulding (2002); Strauss and Corbin (1998)

G

Hh

Hawthorne Effect

The Hawthorne effect is a term generally used to acknowledge the possibility that the presence of the people conducting **research** in a research setting is likely to cause changes in the behaviour of research participants and **respondents**.

The term came into being following a research project conducted at the Hawthorne Plant of the Western Electrical Company (Chicago, USA) (Roethlisberger and Dickson, 1939). The **researchers** set out to see if changes in lighting and temperature in the workplace would have a notable effect on productivity levels. For example, as the lighting was increased and improved, the research hypothesized that productivity would increase (see **hypothesis**). The research was set up with an **experimental design** involving various attempts to set up **control groups**. However, the researchers obtained **data** and findings that they could not readily understand. In essence, as the experiment progressed over time, productivity increased irrespective of the changes and adjustments made by the researchers in the illumination and thermal conditions. Further experiments and adjustments were trialled but productivity continued to climb.

Examination and explanation for these events pointed up issues for not only the specific research project but research in general. The researchers realized that something else, beyond the **variables** they had focused on, was taking place. It was recognized and concluded that, among other things, the research participants had in fact responded to what they saw as an enhancement of their **identity** by being selected for the trial. In other words, the workers were enjoying the attention and the processes of socially constructing their identities in a positive manner as a consequence (see **social constructionism**). They also interacted and socialized with the researchers, reinforcing this identity change (see Gill and Johnson, 2010, for an extensive presentation on experimental design and the Hawthorne experiments and their implications).

Moreover, the case of the Hawthorne experiments and the subsequent creation and labelling of the *Hawthorne effect* also underlined potential shortcomings and pitfalls in experimental design both in terms of the specific Hawthorne experiments but also in its general methodological approach. Simply stated, it is very challenging to observe complex human social contexts and be able to easily isolate 'variables' and their effect on one another. In a complex and messy social fabric of human society, a multiplicity of factors may be at play at any given time in a given social setting (Monahan and Fisher, 2010; Stovall, 2010).

Key Words
Control Groups, Data, Experimental Design, Hypothesis, Respondents, Variable

References
Gill and Johnson (2010); Monahan and Fisher (2010); Stovall (2010)

Hermeneutics

Hermeneutics is concerned with and involves processes of interpretation. It was originally associated with the interpretation of religious texts (see, only by way of illustration, Jensen, 2007; or Pilarski, 2011). However, it has come to be applied to a wider range of writing in the contemporary era. Hermeneutics is a term that is now applied to text, **discourse**, acts, behaviour, speech, signs, symbols, and so on and so forth, indeed anything that it is possible to subject to processes of interpretation. The fact that events and phenomena are considered open to interpretation inherently means that their meaning is not believed to be fixed, given or preordained. In relation to this the social, cultural and historical **contexts** surrounding the artefact or phenomena being interpreted are very significant. Equally, the act of **interpreting** is not neutral and the person undertaking the interpretation will have their own values and background that influence what sense is made of the text or materials. This interactive and ongoing process is sometimes referred to as the *hermeneutic cycle* (Driver, 2008; Hansen, 2006; Prasad, 2002).

It is not uncommon in **research methodology** texts to see an author refer to data **analysis** being 'conducted in a hermeneutic manner'. When the text is examined more closely it is frequently the case that the rather technical sounding term of hermeneutics is

H

being used as a synonym for analysing and **interpreting** the text in a close manner.

Key Words
Interpretation, Text, Discourse

References
Driver (2008); Hansen (2006); Jensen (2007); Pilarski (2011); Prasad (2002)

Histogram

A histogram is a form of chart or diagram. Most importantly, the columns or blocks representing the **variables** and **data** of the **research** are charted in proportion to the surface area. A key feature of the data being charted is that they are continuous in nature: therefore, where the charting of one category of data ends the next leads on from it. In other words, there are no spaces or gaps along the bottom axis of a histogram because in some greater or lesser regard the axis represents data values (see Saunders, Lewis and Thornhill, 2007; Woods, 2007 for further indications).

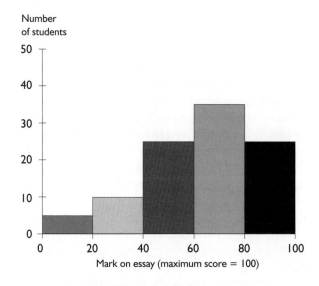

Figure 2 An example of a histogram

A histogram is different and contrasts from, for example, a **bar chart**. A bar chart plots separate columns of data along the base, and the height of the column is the straightforward **frequency** (count or number) of that category of data.

Key Words
Data, Frequency, Variable

References
Saunders, Lewis and Thornhill (2007); Woods (2007)

Hypothesis (*plural* Hypotheses)

A hypothesis can be described as a provisional or suggested explanation of a situation or issue. If proven as valid or correct, it becomes possible to acknowledge the proposal as constituting a '**truth**' or 'fact'.

Hypotheses are a central aspect of, for example, a positivistic scientific experimentalist approach to creating **knowledge** wherein a given hypothesis might be proved correct or incorrect (see **positivism**, **experimental design** and **epistemology**). Even an invalid or incorrect hypothesis is valuable because it can show the **researcher** *what is not the case* as well as what is the case and thereby better paints the overall picture and appreciation of the field. Hypotheses are also employed in more interpretivistic and **qualitative** research but here, rather than trying to *prove* the hypothesis correct or incorrect, it is more often a question of generating description and understanding around the hypothetical proposition (see **interpretivism**).

In business management and organization **research**, it is common to find hypotheses predominantly used in certain domains. For example, forms of positivistic research are commonly considered the normative approach among North American academics and most of the highly ranked journals expect papers to follow this style of **research methodology**. European (and UK) journals tend to encourage research from a broader span of interpretivistic and positivistic style methodologies (see **interpretivism** and **positivism**).

H

Key Words
Epistemology, Interpretivism, Positivism, Theory, Truth

References
Bryman and Bell (2007); Miettinen and Virkkunen (2005)

Identity

Discussions on the nature of identity have been a recurrent theme in philosophy and the social sciences (see, by way of illustration, writings by Plato (428–327 BCE), Leibniz (1646–1716), Hume (1711–1776), Locke (1632–1704) and Wittgenstein (1889–1951)).

Identity is a central **concept** in business, management and organization studies and **research**. It embraces issues of particular or distinctive characteristics, attributes, values and beliefs, **ethics**, and politics that a person or entity possesses and exhibits.

Identity is widely researched through both inductive and deductive-style approaches. However, because of the complex and social nature of the issues surrounding identity, some **researchers** believe that it tends to be inductive, interpretive studies that are perhaps better suited to provide rich and meaningful data on this domain (see **deductivism**, **inductivism**, **interpretivism**).

Key Words
Deductivism, Ethics, Inductivism, Interpretivism, Politics

References
Du Gay and Elliott (2008); Fineman, Gabriel and Sims (2010); Sims, Pullen and Beech (2007)

Ideographic (*see* Nomothetic)

Inductivism

Inductivism is a methodological approach wherein the **researcher** undertakes **data collection** on a relatively limited or small sample in relation to a **research** topic or area. Subsequently, data **analysis** is conducted through a range of possible approaches. These could include, for example, **Grounded Theory**-style **coding**, **content analysis**, **narrative** and **storytelling** and so on. Alternatively expressed, inductivistic approaches start with a body of **data** and from this develop and establish **concepts** and theoretical frameworks (see **theory**). (It should be noted that this contrasts with approaches using **deductivism** which tend to start with a **theory** or **hypothesis** and test it by gathering data using various structured manners and **research methods**.)

A further important point to note in adopting an inductivist stance is with regard to its view on **ontology**, or the nature of reality, and how it evolves and is formed. For inductivist approaches, **subjectivity** plays, to a greater or lesser extent, a central role in understanding what is ultimately considered 'to be the case' or 'to exist' or not. Rather than seeing 'facts', 'events' and phenomena at face value or as a given, inductive approaches are interested in how **respondents** and actors in the **research** setting undertake, for instance, **sensemaking** or social constructive processes in order to account for their experiences (see **lived experience** and **social constructionism**). Research approaches espousing inductivism are often conducted under the umbrella of **interpretivism**.

If an inductive approach has been adopted for a piece of research then, given the subjectivity inherently present, the researcher also needs to appreciate that he or she is playing a role in producing the data, data analysis and ultimate findings. This idea is encapsulated in the notion of **reflexivity** (Alvesson and Sköldberg, 2009). Here, in **writing up** the account of the research, it is important for the researcher to acknowledge the relationships, interactions, origins of data and conceptual frameworks. In other words, how did all of these emerge and come into being? What happened to create them from within the research and the data? It is equally important to remember that the data come from the respondents as will indications about what is important and significant in that data – commonly stated thoughts, words and ideas by participants and so on and so forth. However, it is the researcher who is **interpreting** all of this and writing up the final account. Inevitably, that cannot be a neutral process but it can be a balanced, well-informed and detailed rendering. It is for this reason that inductive accounts tend to involve substantial and in-depth passages of description and background context. The overall effect is to allow the reader to have enough information and insights to be able to make a judgement concerning the **reliability** and **validity** of the account.

Key Words
Analysis, Context, Data Collection, Hypothesis, Inductivism, Interpretivism, Lived Experience, Objectivity, Reflexivity, Reliability, Respondents, Social Construction-ism, Subjectivity, Validity

References
Bryman and Bell (2007); Jankowicz (2005); Kuhn (2009); Silverman (2010a,b); Whittle (2008)

Information

Information involves the idea of conveying or relaying news, details and **knowledge**. A key distinction to note is that **data** are not necessarily information. Information is what is produced from or as a consequence of data. In this way, the receipt of information allows a **researcher** or other individual to move on to identify possible inferences and implications to be established (Wootton and Horne, 2002).

Key Words
Data, Knowledge, Implication, Inference

References
Wootton and Horne (2002)

Informed Consent (*see* Consent)

Interpreting (Data)

The act and process of interpreting is about distilling and identifying **meaning** and significance in the object, sphere, setting or interaction under consideration. Within a given **context** of **research**, different **research methods** and techniques are likely to be used. In broad terms, with **quantitative** data it is possible to apply a range of, although not exclusively, statistical-style analyses (see **statistics** and **analysis**) (see Curwin and Slater, 2007; Swift and Piff, 2010). On the other hand, **qualitative** data are likely to be analysed and interpreted using techniques that, in essence, involve the **researcher** looking over the **data** for significant recurrences, patterns and incidents and attempting to build a conceptual framework from these.

Typical methods for interpreting qualitative data might include, by way of illustration, (**participant**) **observation, ethnography, Grounded Theory, textual analysis, interview** transcript **analysis, content analysis** (Silverman, 2010a,b).

Of course, under certain circumstances it is possible to see a mixture of the approaches (see, for example, commentaries on this in the *Journal of Mixed Methods Research*). Processes of interpreting data will necessarily invoke the need to establish and demonstrate the **validity, reliability** and **generalizability** of the data findings and conclusions.

Key Words

Analysis, Context, Data, Generalizability, Meaning, Qualitative, Quantitative, Reliability, Validity

References

Curwin and Slater (2007); Silverman (2010a,b); Swift and Piff (2010)

Interpretative Research

Interpretative **research** and **data** are **data collection** processes that use **research methodologies** and methods based on **interpretivism**. Interpretative research is founded on principles of **inductivism**. Among other things, inductivism tends to build **theory** and conceptual frameworks by gathering data and subjecting them to particular techniques of analysis, for example, **Grounded Theory, content analysis** and so on and so forth. In addition, interpretative research sees important roles for, by way of illustration, **subjectivity, reflexivity, sense-making** and **social constructionism**. This form of research sees **meaning** from data being generated by the interactions of research **respondents** in their particular research settings and **contexts**. As a consequence of these, it is possible that multiple 'truths' and interpretations have to be analysed and assessed by the **researcher** (Fisher, 2010: 47–70).

Key Words

Data, Data Collection, Contexts, Inductivism, Meaning, Reflexivity, Respondents, Sense-making, Social Constructionism, Subjectivity

References

Fisher (2010); Silverman (2010a,b)

Interview

An interview is a conversation, an interrogation or an oral exchange with the objective of securing **data** and ultimately **information**. Interviews are an important **research method** and can be conducted via telephone or face to face. Within the general method and process of conducting interviews there are a number of typical phases. The topic or focus of the interviews needs to be established. This will be driven by the research **aims**, **objectives** and overall **research questions**. Suitable and useful questions need to be developed by the **researcher**. These will usually be a combination of **open questions** and **closed questions**. Also, at this stage of planning, thought needs to be given to which techniques of **analysis** will be used on the data. This may well influence decisions in relation to **data collection** itself. It is often a good idea to run a **pilot study** in order to see how the questions work in a live situation.

Following this stage, potential interviewees need to be identified and approached. This might involve a combination of telephone, email, and face-to-face contact. When this has been completed, the interviews need to be planned and a schedule drawn up.

Interviews will typically be structured, semi-structured or unstructured. A *structured interview* will have a list of precise questions that are posed to the interviewee one after another. They are more likely to be closed questions rather than open questions. This leaves little or no space or latitude for the interviewees to expand or develop responses. This form of interview may be useful when the interviewer wishes simply to secure similar key information from a number of people. A variation on the structured interview is the *semi-structured interview*. This also has a number of key questions that will be asked to every person interviewed. However, some of these questions may be open questions, which affords the interviewee the opportunity to elaborate and talk at some length on issues. These sorts of answers are often more challenging to analyse but they can provide richer and more in-depth insights. Quite often they will indicate why the interviewee answered 'yes' or 'no' to earlier closed questions. Finally, it is possible to have *unstructured interviews*. Therein, the interview is likely to commence with the interviewer indicating a general theme or question and the interview flowing on from that point as, more or less, a conversation. These forms of interview can potentially provide very powerful insights and extensive descriptive and complex detail.

Because of this they can also be challenging, but nevertheless rewarding, to analyse (see Fisher, 2010: 167–72 for useful tips on carrying out interviews, in addition to King and Horrocks, 2010; and Kvale, 2007).

Key Words
Analysis, Closed Questions, Data, Data Collection, Ethics, Information, Open Questions, Pilot Study

References
Fisher (2010); King and Horrocks (2010); Kvale (2007)

Introduction

In the **context** of a **research** document, be it an article, a **thesis** or other materials, an introduction is the initial and preliminary section that presents and opens the overall **discussion**. Introductions have the potential to be very important and informative in terms of 'scene-setting' or placing a work in context.

In terms of format, usually an introduction will provide some form of very general and broad recent historical background leading up to the contemporary setting in relation to the topic to be discussed in the main document. Then, it will move from this general approach in order to concentrate on the specific or focal literature and issues that the document is concerned with. The introduction will often indicate some of the steps or stages that will be undertaken in order to explore the issues and some of the central points to be investigated. It usually ends without providing a firm conclusion but rather opens out towards the first section or chapter of the work that is to follow. Perhaps a contemporary metaphor for an introduction is, to some extent, that of a trailer for a film at the cinema. This shows the audience the general nature of the film and some of the things that take place during it. However, it does not reveal the ending. In the same way as an introduction, a film trailer aims to engage and entice the reader to go further with the experience.

Introductions are often confused with **abstracts.** Abstracts are more like miniature, condensed versions of the overall work in that they explicitly reveal the theme; the way it has been treated by the literature and **methodology** and the **data** and findings that have been identified and the implications for future research (Hart, 1998, 2004; Jesson and Matheson, 2011; Ridley, 2008).

Key Words
Abstract, Context, Data, Thesis

References
Hart (1998, 2004); Jesson and Matheson (2011); Ridley (2008)

Iterative

Iterative means repetitious, frequent or recurrent. In **research** it is often used as a general, rather than a particularly specific, term. It indicates an approach to research that is not necessarily completely worked out at the beginning of the research project. An iterative approach employs a range of **methods** and commences **data collection**. Then as the process progresses and some analyses of the **data** have taken place, the **researcher** may, based on these initial indications, decide to adjust the research approach and methods. In other words, one event or insight by the researcher may lead him or her to create or elect another action or direction (Kerssens-van Drongelen, 2001).

This approach can be used in a number of situations and **contexts** including, for example, the **pilot study** phase of a project where techniques and methods are being tested and tried out. Although there is of course potential to factor an iterative phase into any research project, it is perhaps more likely to play a role in an inductive and interpretative-style approach that is tending to take its sense and direction from the **respondents** and the research field rather than following a predetermined process and programme (as would be more likely the case with, for example, **experimental design**) (see **inductivism, interpretivism**).

Key Words
Data, Data Collection, Context, Experimental Design, Inductivism, Interpretivism, Pilot Study

References
Kerssens-van Drongelen (2001)

Knowledge

Knowledge is a complex **concept** which has attracted a considerable amount of comment over the centuries. Knowledge concerns awareness and familiarity with a subject or topic. When we use the term *knowledge* it is often linked to the notion of providing **information**. The term knowledge also conveys the notion of an overall body or collection of things that are understood in relation to an issue or subject.

From some points of view, the notion of knowledge might suggest a body of ideas and thoughts that exist 'out there' and are coded and logged for all to see. However, it is important to appreciate that knowledge is developed, emerges and ultimately 'is made'. For **research methodology,** knowledge and how knowledge comes into being (that is, is made or produced) is a centrally important issue. This process is called **epistemology**. Each **research** methodological approach will have its own epistemological characteristics (see **research methodology**). For example, a positivistic, deductive approach will tend to see 'facts', 'events' and so on and so forth as being to some greater or lesser extent already formed and ready to be subjected to examination and exploration through **experimental design** (see **positivism** and **deductivism**). Alternatively, an interpretivistic and inductive approach is more likely to see 'facts' and 'events' as being in emergent formation – a consequence of social interaction (see **interpretivism** and **inductivism**). Both inductive and deductive approaches produce 'knowledge' but that knowledge has been produced in very different and contrasting ways.

In organization and management studies, there have been extensive discussions on the concept and nature of 'knowledge' (see, for example, Robertson and Swan, 2004; Spender and Scherer, 2007).

Key Words
Deductivism, Epistemology, Experimental Design, Inductivism, Interpretivism, Positivism, Research Methodology

References
Robertson and Swan (2004); Spender and Scherer (2007)

K

Language

Language is an aspect of processes and means of communication. The subject and sphere encompassed by language are vast and broach a range of domains and disciplines including linguistics, philosophy and sociology. Moreover, language is often discussed in relation to the **concept** and field(s) of **discourse**, which has emerged as an important dimension of some approaches to business management and organization (see, for example, Taylor and Robichaud, 2004; Tietze, Cohen and Musson, 2003).

Research methodology discussions on language are prone to adopting diverse approaches. For positivistic methodological approaches, discussions centring on language will tend to view utterances at broadly face value (see **positivism** and **deductivism**). This will typically provide, for example, **respondent data** that test and explore a given **hypothesis.** In contrast, more interpretivistic and inductive approaches are likely to employ **research methods** and techniques that are concerned with considering ways in which language and discourse can be, for example, deconstructed or socially constructed in shifting and emergent processes (see **deconstructionism, social constructionism**). **Narrative research** and storytelling may play a role in this (Grant, Hardy and Putnam, 2011a,b,c; Hardy, 2004).

Key Words
Data, Deconstructionism, Deductivism, Discourse, Hypothesis, Narrative Research, Positivism, Research Methods, Respondent, Social Constructionism, Storytelling

References
Grant, Hardy and Putnam (2011a,b,c); Hardy (2004); Taylor and Robichaud (2004); Tietze, Cohen and Musson (2003)

Likert Rating Scale

A Likert rating scale is a way of asking **respondents** and **research** participants to make a personal judgement or **evaluation** regarding a topic or issue. Likert scales are most commonly used as a **data collection** method in conjunction with **questionnaires** and, on occasion, structured **interviews.**

Examples of a Likert scale would be:

I am motivated in my job.

| *Strongly agree* | *Agree* | *Undecided* | *Disagree* | *Strongly disagree* |

I am well paid.

| *Strongly agree* | *Agree* | *Undecided* | *Disagree* | *Strongly disagree* |

Alternative examples might include:

| *Poor* | *Acceptable* | *Average* | *Good* | *Excellent* |
| *Never* | *Rarely* | *Occasionally* | *Often* | *Very frequently* |

This form of data collection can lend itself well to statistical and **quantitative analysis** (see **statistics**).

Key Words
Analysis, Data Collection, Interview, Questionnaire

References
Sapsford (2006); Wilson (2010)

L

Line Graph

A line graph is a diagram with axes that uses a line to show how a particular item or entity (represented as a **variable**) moves and changes over a period of time. For example, a line graph could be used to illustrate the changing level or value of inflation over time. On the vertical axis would be charted 'inflation rate' measured as a percentage and on the horizontal axis would be time measured in days, months or years (Steinberg, 2010; Wallgren, 1996).

Key Words
Variable

References
Steinberg (2010); Wallgren (1996).

Linear

The term *linear* relates to lines and the characteristics of lines. In the arena of **research methodology**, 'linear' is most directly associated with things such as graphs and statistical charting (see **statistics**) in that lines are often used to represent and present **data**.

The act of referring to something as 'linear' may also be used by more interpretivistic accounts in order to distinguish those approaches from deductive approaches and their linear features (see **interpretivism**). It may occasionally be used in a slightly pejorative sense in that inductive approaches are less prone to categorizing and delineating data in the ways that deductive processes engage (see **deductivism**). For inductive approaches, avoidance of linearity is seen as affording an opportunity to engage the subjective and emergent aspects of data whereas for deductive processes, linearity offers clear constructs and boundaries around which objective observations and comment can be made (see **inductivism** and **subjectivity**) (Alvesson and Deetz, 2000).

Key Words
Data, Deductivism, Inductivism, Interpretivism, Research Methodology, Subjectivity

References
Alvesson and Deetz (2000)

Linear Regression

This is a mathematical technique used to chart the relationship between two types of **data** or **variables**. This is grounded in **statistics** and statistical techniques. The use of the approach enables a **researcher** to see how closely related (or not) the two variables are. One of the variables will be a dependent variable that responds and reflects changes in an independent variable; for example, how dependent productivity output is on changes in wage levels. **Linear** regression also employs tests that indicate the closeness of the

L

relationship between the variables and the degree to which changes in one variable can be considered to be coincidental or causal (Wright and London, 2009).

Key Words
Data, Researcher, Statistics, Variable

References
Wright and London (2009)

Literature Review

A literature review is typically the section of a **research** paper, **dissertation** or **thesis** that considers the writing that other authors have already produced on the topic. A literature review may also occasionally be referred to as a *literature search* or a *critical literature review.* This latter term or label highlights that the central aim of a review is to critique, analyse, compare and contrast various writings on a given area.

Although not obligatory, it is often a good idea to commence your literature review with the literature dealing with some of the background or *historical* **context** to the issue(s) being considered. This sets the scene and allows the review to lead on the literature that goes on to address the *contemporary* situation and issues in relation to that background context.

The decision regarding which bodies of literatures are to be looked at will be determined by a combination of the **title** of the work, the **aims** and **objectives** and the **research questions**. Within the title of the work there will be referents or nouns. For example, a dissertation could have the title:

An Analysis of Critical Factors Influencing Merger and Acquisition Activity in the Swiss Pharmaceutical Industry 1960–2011

With regard to the literature review it would be reasonable to anticipate that at least two of the areas for which literature would need to be sought are:

The Swiss Pharmaceutical Industry 1960–2011
and
Mergers and Acquisition

The body of literature on the *Swiss Pharmaceutical Industry* would probably commence with an overall view of the pharmaceutical industry in the world context, since this is an industry of a particularly global nature. The discussion could then focus on the specific Swiss context in relation to the preceding examination of the overall global context. Then, following on from this, the author may elect to discuss the body of literature on *mergers and acquisitions*. In a similar manner to the discussion on the pharmaceutical industry, this would most likely commence by examining globally relevant literature on mergers and acquisitions and then concentrate on material more directly relevant to the Swiss context.

Alternatively, depending on how the work was shaped, the author might start with a general discussion on mergers and acquisitions, the focus on mergers and acquisitions in the pharmaceutical industry and, subsequently, focus on a case study of the Swiss context.

In this brief illustration a number of typical and generic underlying principles for literature reviews can be seen:

- Literature reviews will generally have a general *background* literature base and also a more *focal* specific literature base (Phillips and Pugh, 2010).
- Following on from this, literature reviews tend to move from the general to the specific.
- In parallel with the above two principles, literature reviews tend to provide historical **context** first and then present the contemporary situation in relation to this.
- More technically, we can see from the above three points that, drawing on the field of *pragmastylistics* (the study of choice and use of language), we can see that in formal and academic writing *new* **information** *nearly always follows old information* (Hickey, 1993; Hickey and Stewart, 2005). In other words, first we say something about a topic and then we tend to say something further about what we have just mentioned. This idea operates in relations between major sections of the work (for example background and focal literatures). It also flows through the smaller sections and units of writing that make up these bigger sections. This includes, for example, subheaded sections and the paragraphs within them and even the relationship between the sentences within any given paragraph. In this way, sense and understanding are slowly built up by the author for the reader. If the reader ever has a sense of getting lost in the text then it is

L

almost always the case that the writer has undermined the logic outlined above. Metaphorically speaking, the writer 'let go of the reader's hand' and 'surprised or shocked him or her'. Such instances might be entirely appropriate, indeed desirable, in writing something like a novel where intrigue and suspense are required, but not in a formal piece of academic writing where progressive logic and reasoning are needed.

With regard to searching for the literature, this, in turn, raises the issue of *search terms*. These are the terms that a **researcher** uses to search databases. Your initial search terms will almost certainly come from your title and aims and objectives. Drawing on the example above, an initial listing might include: 'mergers', 'acquisitions', 'pharmaceutical (industry)' or pharmaceutics, and 'Swiss (industry)'. This will produce a breadth of material that will need to be skimmed and sifted through. At this stage it is best not to read too many things in depth. Rather, it is better to note that they are potentially valuable and keep a copy of the document, or at least the reference, accompanied by a note reminding you of why you felt it was useful. Following on from this initial trawl you are likely to be satisfied with what some of the search terms have generated but not others. In other words, some of the information will be highly relevant and other information will be too general or simply not relevant enough. However, any material might give you a clue to a new search term that will identify a very interesting seam of literature to be mined. Sometimes these might be constituted of synonyms for terms you have already used or alternatively they might be entirely new terms. Using the example above, synonyms for mergers and acquisition might be 'industrial concentration' or 'industrial consolidation'. Fresh search terms that emerge from a new search might variously centre on 'transformation', 'transition', 'change management', 'leadership' in the pharmaceutical industry. When similar or recurrent information starts to emerge from these searches it is probable that you have gone as far as you are able to with the search terms you are employing.

In relation to writing a literature review it should be remembered that it is not simply a reiteration or description of the literature that is 'out there'. Writing a literature review is about the researcher and author of that review establishing where he or she stands in relation to that literature. This means that as a consequence of reading the literature, the writer/researcher needs to decide whether or not he or she agrees with what other authors have found and proposed. This is the way that an *argument* is gradually built up. Often students may not have particularly strong views on a particular academic issue or model. It is, in large part, precisely for this reason that some students find it hard to produce an argument. To be able to do so means that *you have to believe in something* in order to see whether or not what you are reading fits with, or informs, that belief. A comparison might be to think of political parties and views. It is relatively easy to imagine holding strong opinions on what certain parties and their leaders do and say. It is this sort of political passion (with a small 'p') that needs to be at play when you are doing your literature review.

Equally, in trying to avoid producing a rather descriptive literature review, which will contain little critical analysis, try to remember the following idea triptych: *information, inference, implication*. For each key point or piece of **data** or theme in the literature, first, we need to say 'what is' and offer a presentation of the ideas – this is the *information* stage and by nature it does tend to be rather descriptive. Then the writer/researcher needs to tell the reader what he or she believes should be understood from, and in relation to, the information – what does or would he or she like it to mean/how should it be interpreted? Finally, it is important to say what are the outcomes and consequences of this critique and observations that have been made – this is the 'so what?' question that needs to be answered.

A common question by people undertaking a literature review is 'when will I know I have read or got enough literature?' Alternatively expressed, when will enough literature be sufficient for the purposes of the work? It is important for a researcher to appreciate and understand that it will always be very challenging, if not impossible, to summarize or encapsulate everything that has been written on a given topic. There is simply too much being written at any given period of time and it is constantly being added to, and built on, the research and work that has preceded it. With the advent of the internet and electronic publishing, this dilemma has grown to an even greater extent. In response to this issue, a useful metaphor is to think of literature as a wide, deep and fast-flowing never-ending river. It is continuous and all that can ever be done is to aim to assess the dimensions of the river at a given point in time. The moment this has been done the water in the river has already flowed on and the river's details and characteristics have been subjected to minor modifications that gradually, and even sometimes swiftly, will lead to major shifts and changes in the landscape. Literature is little

L

different to this – it is constant in its flow and forever in transformation, and a literature review will, at best, be a photograph or snapshot in time.

A useful assistance in gaining a rapid feel and impression of the scope of the literature on a given topic is to locate journal articles that have extensive reviews of the relevant material on a subject. Indeed, some articles are entirely dedicated to the task of reviewing the literature in a field. A useful publication is the *International Journal of Management Reviews* which is an official journal of the British Academy of Management.

Most **research methodolog**y texts have sections on literature reviews and each has its own useful tips on approaches to be adopted. (For useful illustrations and information see, for example, Hart, 1998, 2004; Maylor and Blackmon, 2005: 95–131; Saunders, Lewis and Thornhill, 2007.)

Key Words
Aims, Background (and Focal) Literature, Dissertation, Objectives, Pragmastylistics, Research Questions, Thesis

References
Fink (2009); Hickey (1993); Hickey and Stewart (2005); Maylor and Blackmon (2005); Phillips and Pugh (2010); Saunders, Lewis and Thornhill (2007); Walden (2009)

Lived Experience

The notion of lived experience centres on attempts to develop a more contextualized and rich appreciation of how a person or group feel and react in relation to everyday life circumstances. An individual or group make continual and ongoing sense of life and the events, structures and relationships that constitute their experiences (see **sense-making**; and also Weick, 1995). Lived experience is interested in portraying organizational life in a manner that contrasts with anodyne and reductionist accounts of management and organizations sometimes found in certain styles of textbooks and articles (see **reductionism**, **causality** and **modernism**). **Language**, stories and **narratives** are often important means of pointing at and illustrating lived experience in action (Eastmond, 2007) (see **narrative research**).

L

Key Words
Narrative, Reductionism, Representation, Sense-making, Stories

References
See Eastmond (2007); Knights and Willmott (1999); McCabe (2007); O'Doherty (2008); Weick (1995); Zhang, Spicer and Hancock (2008) for illustrations of lived experience commentaries

Longitudinal Research

Longitude means length. A longitudinal piece of **research** is one that lasts for a substantial period of time. This period of time may constitute a year or a number of years. The research intention in such a study is to observe, monitor and assess variations and developments in a situation or set of **variables** over a given period of time (see Collis and Hussey, 2009; Menard, 2007). These forms of studies can be excellent at providing detailed and in-depth understanding of phenomena. However, on the other hand, they can be expensive and difficult to maintain as structural changes may be likely to occur in the research setting (for example a government department under study being abolished or relocated) or even the research team's situation (for example changes in personnel or funding).

Key Words
Variable

References
Collis and Hussey (2009); Menard (2007)

L

Mean

The mean is a measure of average used in **statistics**. It is only one measure of average (others include the **mode** and the **median**), although perhaps in the popular mind and everyday speech it is what many people might term 'the average' of a set of figures or numbers.

In more technical **language** it the answer obtained when you add up all the values of a set of **research** observations and divide that number by the number of observations. For example, we could establish the average number of product units sold per month in a company. To do this we take the *actual* sales for each month and add up the twelve totals in a total for sales for the year. Then divide by 12 (the number of months). So, providing a numerical example this would be:

Sales per month:
J-12 , F-16, M-17, A-12, M-18, J-19, J-27, A-14, S-13, O-16, N-16, D-12

Total sales =
12+16+17+12+18+19+27+14+13+16+16+12 = 192 units sold in the year

Mean average number of units sold per month = 192/12 = 16 units

Measures such as the mean tend to be used to a greater extent in research using **experimental design**, deductive and positivistic types of **research methodology** (see **deductivism** and **positivism**). These forms of numerical measure marry well with the principles and commitments of these approaches (that is, **objectivity**, **reductionism**, **causality** and so on and so forth) but they are less useful in inductive, interpretivistic and ethnographic type approaches wherein it is generally felt that 'facts' and 'truths' are better represented by in-depth and rich description and **analysis** (see inductivism, interpretivism and ethnography). Nevertheless, this is not to discount either approach and it is of course possible that a measure such as the mean average may find a role to play in any approach to research (Ha, 2011; Steinberg, 2010).

Key Words
Analysis, Causality, Ethnography, Experimental Design, Inductivism, Interpretivism, Median, Mode, Objectivity, Reductionism, Research Methodology, Statistics

References
Ha (2011); Steinberg (2010)

Meaning

Meaning involves a human process of developing understanding and significance. In conjunction with this, it also concerns how people feel, react, interpret and make sense of stimuli, events, objects and so on and so forth. Meaning constitutes a substantial aspect of the social sciences. To some extent, this contrasts with the natural sciences where the emphasis is on attempts to explore, explain and test physical, chemical and biological processes and perspectives.

In relation to **research methodology**, issues of meaning are central to inductive, interpretive and ethnographic approaches to research (see **inductivism, interpretivism and ethnography**). From these methodological stances, it is generally acknowledged that meaning is produced by research **respondents** and that **researchers** are inevitably part of **sense-making** and **analysis** of these **data**. In this way, meanings are negotiated, emergent and ever-changing based on myriad dimensions of **language**, **discourse**, signs, symbols, stories, metaphors and **narratives** (see **narrative research**). Naturally, such points go to the heart of varying epistemological and ontological positions in various research methodologies (see **epistemology** and **ontology**) (See also Fairhurst, 2004; and Martens, 2006, among many possible others, for illustrations of research working with issues of meaning.)

M

Key Words
Data, Discourse, Epistemology, Ethnography, Inductivism, Interpretivism, Language, Ontology, Narrative Research, Research Methodology, Storytelling

References
Czarniawska (2004); Fairhurst (2004); Martens (2006)

Median

The median is a measure of average used in **statistics**. It is only one measure of average and others include the **mode** and the **mean**. The median indicates the 'mid-point' value in a set of **data**. In other words, if the pieces of data are arranged in order of value and magnitude (that is, size) then there are an equal number of pieces of data below and above the median value. For example, taking once more the illustration of number of units sold per month used in the discussion of the mean average:

Sales per month:
J-12, F-16, M-17, A-12, M-18, J-19, J-27, A-14, S-13, O-16, N-16, D-12

Re-arranging these in size order:
J-12, D-12, A-12, S-13, A-14, F-16, O-16, N-16, M-17, M-18, J-19, J-27

Median average number (or mid-point value) of units sold per month = 16 units

In this example, the median is the same as the mean. However, there is no guarantee that this will always be the case. The comments made in the entry for the **mean** regarding the tendency to use statistical averages (see **statistics**) also apply for the median.

Key Words
Data, Mean, Mode, Statistics

References
Ha (2011); Steinberg (2010)

Meta-analysis

The term *meta-analysis* means a process wherein the results and findings from a number of studies on a particular area are synthesized. This can permit a more holistic overview of the nature and scope of a given area. It is an approach particularly used in **quantitative** methods. However, the term can be used in a generic sense in relation to **qualitative** type work (Cooper, 2009; Fink, 2009; Gelbrich and Roschk, 2011).

Key Words
Qualitative, Quantitative

References
Cooper (2009); Fink (2009); Gelbrich and Roschk (2011); Lux, Crook and Woehr (2011)

Method (*see* Research Methods)

Methodology (*see* Research Methodology)

Mixed Method Research

Mixed method **research** is a potentially interesting idea and approach. However, it is also a term that can provoke some confusion.

The term *mixed methods* appears, at first sight, to allude to issues relating uniquely to research **methods** rather than **methodologies.** However, the term really is concerned with the idea of *mixed methodologies.*

When the term 'mixed methods' is employed, many authors suggest that this means the process of choosing to mix and use both **quantitative** and **qualitative** research approaches within the same piece of research. The implication is that this may introduce some sort of tension or conflict in the work due to the fact that quantitative and qualitative methods and **data** use different processes and have different physical characteristics or nature. These differences are often presented simply as: qualitative approaches tend to use words and description and analyses based on emergent themes on issues; whereas quantitative approaches tend to draw on numbers, and statistical approaches and techniques (see **statistics**). This is, to a certain point valid but, in large part, obscures or overlooks the more complex and important underlying issues.

M

In fact, the situation is better viewed and discussed as follows:

- Firstly, any research *can* contain qualitative and/or quantitative *data*. However, it is indeed something of a misnomer to say that 'I am doing a quantitative **dissertation**' or alternatively 'I am doing a qualitative dissertation' as students commonly say. This is because it is *research methodology* that determines the *nature* of the research rather than *methods* (see also in conjunction with the entries for **research method** and **research methodology**).
- Thus, a research project attempting to combine, inductive and deductive research methodologies (see **deductivism** and **inductivism**) will have great difficulties. This is because, in terms of the epistemological and ontological views and characteristics underpinning these approaches, inductivism and deductivism pull in opposite directions (see **epistemology** and **ontology**).
- This is because, **inductivism** sees the world as emergent, and constructed through **subjectivity** and **sense-making** that involves **language**, signs, symbols and **discourse** in the **context**(s) in which the **respondent**(s) is living and acting. Samples in inductive research tend to be quite small and localized (for example a limited number of cases) and the internal **validity** and **reliability** of these is assured through in-depth descriptive analytical comment based on respondent-provided data (see **sampling**). It tends not to be possible for this type of research to be easily more widely generalized because it values the fact that its findings are intrinsically rooted in a specific setting or context.
- However, **deductivism** sees the world as fixed, stable and essentially 'out there' waiting to be explored, discovered, categorized and 'labelled' (see **representation**). This process of understanding is undertaken by designing research based on **experimental design**, **positivism** and kindred approaches which value objective quantification, measurement and the repeated testing of generalized **hypotheses** against a wide range of cases so as to be able to ensure the widely generalized validity and reliability of the research (see **objectivity**). In order to facilitate this, the sample is likely to be quite large.
- Therefore, in summary, taking the two broad approaches to research outlined above, when the term 'mixed methods' is employed by a **researcher** to mean that that there will be an attempt to use a combination of inductive (for example

M

interpretivism) and deductive (for example **positivism**) approaches (see **inductivism** and **deductivism**), these are actually incompatible. This situation is often described as *paradigm incommensurability*. In other words, these methodological **paradigms** simply have conflicting principles and value bases and it is, to adapt a well-known phrase, 'like trying to make a marriage of chalk and cheese' – attempting to mix inductive and deductive (often inaccurately termed respectively simply as 'phenomenological' and 'positivist' in a range of texts) is just not possible (see **positivism** and **phenomenology**).

- As a final further point to note, it is perfectly possible, although not in every situation, to use mixed *methods* (as opposed to **(research) methodologies**). For example, the manner in which a researcher uses **interviews, questionnaires, focus groups** and **content analysis** and so on and so forth will be guided and shaped in terms of design, conduct and **analysis** needs and dictates of the overall research methodology being used (see the entries on **interviews** and **questionnaires** for detailed commentary on how these might vary). Using a range of methods in a piece of research can add value and strength to the work. It can produce different data in range of ways. If so desired it can also be used in **triangulation** processes to cross check data and reinforce validity and reliability (however, some commentators have philosophical reservations about trying to triangulate inductive studies – see **inductivism** and **triangulation**). (See by way of overall illustration Clark and Creswell, 2008; Creswell and Clark, 2010; Plowright, 2010.)

Key Words
Deductivism, Inductivism, Method, Objectivity, Paradigm, Positivism, Reliability, Research Methodology, Subjectivity, Validity

References
Clark and Creswell (2008); Creswell and Clark (2010); Plowright (2010).
The *Journal of Mixed Methods Research* is a useful generic publication to consult.

Mode

The mode is a measure of average used in **statistics**. It is only one measure of average and others include the **mean** and the **median**. The mode indicates the most commonly recurring **data** value in a set of data. In other words, if the data are arranged in clusters within which the pieces of data have the same value then the mode puts the question – 'which data value cluster had the most pieces of data in it?' Colloquially put – 'which bucket has the most in?' For example, taking again the illustration of number of units sold per month used in the discussion of the mean average:

Sales per month:
J-12, F-16, M-17, A-12, M-18, J-19, J-27, A-14, S-13, O-16, N-16, D-12

Re-arranging these in clusters of months having the same number of sales:
J-12, D-12, A-12
S-13
A-14
F-16, O-16, N-16
M-17
M-18
J-19
J-27

In this particular example it so happens that there are, in fact, two modes, 12 and 16. This is actually called a *bimodal* (that is, two modes) **distribution**. If the data were different, for example February had something like 13 in instead of 16, then this would leave the clear modal value as 12.

The comments made in the entry for the **mean** regarding the tendency to use statistical averages (see **statistics**) also apply for the mode.

Key Words
Data, Mean, Median, Statistics

References
Ha (2011); Steinberg (2010)

Modernism (*also* Modernity)

Modernism is a philosophy and a movement that takes the **concept** of **rationalism** as a central principle. As such it values **objectivity**, and **linear representations** of events and objects. Modernism finds its roots and origins in a broad range of British and European continental philosophers who were part of the Enlightenment of the seventeenth and eighteenth centuries including René Descartes (1596–1650), Voltaire (1694–1778), Rousseau (1712–1778) Diderot (1713–1784), Adam Smith (1723–1790), David Hume (1711–1776) and Sir Isaac Newton (1642–1727). In its desire for objective **knowledge** engaged with the new and emerging ideas of science, modernism embraced **experimental design** and **positivism**.

Modernism continues to be a dominant conceptual pattern of thinking in many parts and aspects of the Western world. It is generally considered to have been at its most potent and widespread in the late nineteenth and early twentieth centuries. Modernism has become the generic term that represents the manner in which this rationalistic ideology was applied to a range of fields and significant contributors include inter alios: Le Corbusier (1887–1965) in architecture, Joyce (1882–1941) in literature, Kandinsky (1866–1944) in painting and Duchamp (1887–1968) in conceptual art (see **rationalism**). All of these fused modernistic principles, and scientific and technological approaches and appreciations into their work (Dereli and Stokes, 2007). Contemporary accounts of management and organizations often continue to be premised on modernistic assumptions, producing presentations and discussions that purport to be logical, rational and objective (see **rationalism** and **objectivity**). Nevertheless, they are likely to be less effective at taking account of more 'messy problems', and **subjectivity** in organizations.

Research methodology does not generally explicitly acknowledge the presence of modernism even though it has influenced and continues to shape large areas of business management and organizational **research** and commentary. It is primarily through the employment of positivistic-style methodologies that this can be evidenced (see **positivism**). In some communities of management academic research and writing, positivistic approaches are seen as orthodoxy. For example, in North America a wide selection of journals that are considered by many to be leading publications accept predominantly statistically, numerically and quantitatively underpinned positivistic-style submissions (see **statistics**, **quantitative** and **positivism**). In contrast, a large swathe, even a majority of, for example, Scandinavian academic work and publishing has a preference for less modernistic and more interpretivistic work (see **interpretivism**). Moreover, the UK, with its tendency to be influenced by

M

US practice, has a spread of modernistic and non- or counter-modernistic writing and research. However, there is concern in some quarters that the trend is to follow the US model in a more earnest manner.

Key Words
Experimental Design, Linear, Objectivity, Positivism, Rationalism, Subjectivity

References
Dereli and Stokes (2007)

Narrative Research

In the most basic terms, narrative is similar to story (although some of the literature offers differences of nuance) in that it is the telling or relaying of a series events by a person or persons. In the past two decades narrative has become increasingly omnipresent and commented on as a both a **methodology** and **method** in business management and organizational **research** (see, by way of example, the work of Boje, 2001; Bold, 2011; Czarniawska, 1998, 2002, 2003, 2004; and Gabriel, 2000). However, this work draws on a range of historical work from other domains in the social science sphere including philosophy, sociology and history (in relation to the earlier mentioned sources see, for example, the recent debate in Wilson and Toms, 2010, in the area of Business History writing; and by way of holistic association, see also **archival research**).

    Data collection that focuses on narratives and stories enables the **researcher** to portray and render research settings and contexts in a vibrant and lively way that illustrates the **lived experience** of the **respondents** and researcher in terms of **reflexivity** (see Stokes and McCulloch, 2006). Narrative is typically used with an inductive, interpretivistic **frame of reference** (see **inductivism** and **interpretivism**).

Key Words
Frame of Reference, Inductivism, Interpretivism, Lived Experience, Method, Methodology, Reflexivity

References
Boje (2001); Bold (2011); Czarniawska (1998, 2002, 2003, 2004); Gabriel (2000); Stokes and McCulloch (2006); Wilson and Toms (2010)

Nomothetic

Nomothetic is a term drawn from, among others, the work of the German philosopher Immanuel Kant (1724–1804) and in the contemporary era is particularly used in psychology (McKenna, 2000). It means the general rules and universal categories that, typically the natural sciences, attempt to develop objective approaches and criteria in order to explain phenomena (see **objectivity**). In other words, it is a highly technical, and not commonly used, phrase whose **meaning** and intent is that it is aligned with characteristics such as **deductivism** and **positivism** as opposed to **inductivism** and **interpretivism**.

The opposite of nomothetic is *ideographic*. This latter term focuses on specific cases and particular contexts rather than generalized and universal rules.

Key Words
Deductivism, Inductivism, Interpretivism, Objectivity, Positivism

References
McKenna (2000)

Normal Distribution

The term normal **distribution** is an expression employed in statistical and graphic analyses and presentations of **data** (see **analysis** and **data**). 'In a perfect normal distribution' means that the **mode**, **mean** and **median** average measures of a given sample have similar values. An example of data that could be charted in this way might be rates of pay for everyone in an organization.

When shown diagrammatically, this means that the graph shows a bell-shaped curve moving from left to right along the bottom axis of the graph. This means that most of the data and values are clustered in the centre of the graph with half the remaining values below them and half the values above them. Often a data sample will not have a normal distribution but will be what is termed *skewed* to the left or the right. A skew towards the left would mean that the average salary tends towards lower values and a skew to the right shows a trend towards higher pay values (Ha, 2011; Steinberg, 2010; Wilson, 2010).

Key Words
Analysis, Data, Mean, Median, Mode, Sample

References
Ha (2011); Steinberg (2010); Wilson (2010)

Note-taking

Note-taking is the process whereby the **researcher** personally records observations and discussions in relation to the **research** project. This might be in relation to, for example, the **literature review** phase or alternatively in the field with research **respondents** (see, for example, Cameron and Price, 2009: 167–70; Denzin, 2008).

It is often useful to reflect on how notes are to be taken and to adopt a pattern or framework for this before entering the field or beginning to read literature. For example, some authors recommend the idea of an annotated bibliography whereby each reference has a brief overview regarding the relevance and interest of the paper to the particular research project in hand.

In the field, when the researcher is conducting, for example, **interviews** and observations, recording with video or a recorder will sometimes not be possible. In this case note-taking is imperative. Indeed, even if recording in some format is possible, taking supplementary notes can be useful for underlining a particular point or event. Note-taking is not perfect or flawless and the notes taken will only ever be an indicative account of the reality experienced (Collis and Hussey, 2009: 192–4; Raleigh-Yow, 1994).

Key Words
Interview, Literature Review, Respondent

N

References
Cameron and Price (2009); Collis and Hussey (2009); Denzin (2008); Raleigh-Yow (1994)

Oo

Objectives

An objective is a desired point of arrival, achievement or attainment. Objectives therefore shape journeys by showing the distance and direction in which to travel. Objectives are an essential and integral part of any **research** project or piece of work. Objectives are nearly always expressed at the beginning or in the early part of the project or research. This allows the rest of the work to be shaped and configured in relation to the objectives. Objectives are usually designed and conceived within overall **aims** (Cameron and Price, 2009: 201; Fisher, 2010).

Objectives should be expressed in practical terms and state clearly the steps that are going to be taken. In doing this, it is useful to remember the oft-used SMART acronym as an *aide memoire*.

Specific   – make them very focused and clear

Measured   – gauge and assess their magnitude and resources required

Attainable   – make sure that they are they possible and achievable

Relevant   – are they on target? Do they fit with the overall aim?

Time-framed – schedule and timings: how long will things take?

This acronym does not need to be shown explicitly in the objectives but it is a helpful handrail for the process of shaping useful and appropriate direction for a piece of research. An example (among the many possible ones) of objectives within research is shown below simply for illustration purposes.

> **Aim:**
> *The aim of this research is to examine the role, relevance and sustainability of outdoor management development courses.*
>
> **Objectives:**
> 1 To conduct an in-depth critical review of the outdoor management literature with particular focus on the nature, relationships and durability of outdoor management development courses.
> 2 To conduct field research consisting of seven case studies of outdoor management development programmes.
> 3 To analyse the field data findings in conjunction with the literature findings and to attempt to reconceptualize a relevant and sustainable theoretical framework for outdoor management development in the future.

Key Words
Aim (see also **research question**)

References
Cameron and Price (2009); Fisher (2010)

Objectivity

A situation or an opinion is said to have objectivity when it is seen to be free and independent from particular prejudice, or partial *emotions* or sentiments. When someone or something displays these characteristics he, she or it is said to show *objectivity*.

In research methodologies, objectivity is a central principle of the scientific approach and **experimental design** to building **knowledge** (see also **epistemology**) and a core element of **positivism** and **modernism**. For adherents of these approaches, knowledge thus created is said to contain, in the sense of the field of **research methodology**, **truth** and **validity**. This way of perceiving the world is underpinned by the notion that reality 'exists out there' independent of, and external to, the mind and body of the observer or **researcher**. Truth and validity have an ontological solidity separate from the person observing or experiencing it (see **ontology**).

In contrast to deductive approaches discussed above, inductive and interpretative approaches have a commitment and belief in the role of **subjectivity** in research settings and interactions between researchers and respondents (**deductivism**, **inductivism** and **interpretivism**) (Couvalis, 1997; Hammersley, 2011).

O

Key Words
Deductivism, Emotion, Epistemology, Experimental Design, Inductivism, Interpretivism, Knowledge, Ontology, Truth, Validity

References
Couvalis (1997); Hammersley (2011)

Observational (*see* Participant Observation)

Ontology (*adjective:* Ontological)

Ontology is a branch of philosophy that is concerned with differing views on the nature of 'reality' and of states of 'being'. In other words, it is about the study of the nature of existence and the assumptions we make about it. It might seem strange to question the nature of reality; after all, to our *empirical* senses, reality might seem clear, uncomplicated and self-evident in so many ways. For example, we feel heat or cold with our skin, we smell a nice or unpleasant odour with our nose, and certain objects apparently self-evidently exist – houses, walls, cars, people, planes and so on and so forth. However, there *are* differing and alternative views concerning what reality might consist of in relation to experiences and phenomena. Different sensations might be associated with different reactions and emotions for different people. Reality varies, for example, through individual perception. What might seem a 'fact' to one person is not necessarily apparent or acceptable as a 'fact' to another individual. An everyday illustration of this might be contrasting views people hold about religion or politics. Some individuals may hold beliefs that will not be valid or constitute 'facts' for other individuals or groups. As such, one person's *view* of reality constituted by 'facts' (and the consequent actions he or she takes following these beliefs) will not necessarily be another person's view or construction of reality and 'facts'.

Within **research** work, it is important to understand and appreciate that all methodological approaches have an ontological standpoint (as well as being set in an **epistemological** tradition). The ontological assumptions of the **researcher** and the researched people and settings play a central role in determining the perceived reality and status of time and space in which they exist. This of course will have an obvious impact on the conduct of the research and subsequent findings. Reality will be *accepted* or *made* in different ways by different individuals.

One way of developing an understanding of ontological positions is to imagine an approximate spectrum stretching, from one end – a position of **realism** that espouses **objectivity** – to the other end, a position of **relativism,** aligned with **subjectivity**. This is, of course, a rather basic **representation** of the situation but it is helpful as a starting point for discussion. From a realist stance for example, scientists employing **positivistic** methodologies see reality and ontology as solid, fixed, permanent and, most importantly, *external* and *objective* to them. This 'external' notion is central to their beliefs. In essence, whether or not they are engaged with, or in close proximity to the object, touching and observing it (even being in the same physical space as it), they believe that the object will exist and be present in just the same way whether or not they are present. This is aligned with *objectivism* and the separation of the things and people (that is, research and researchers) from the researchers themselves. Two aspects that are very important in these processes are representationalism and nominalism**.** In short, these are concerned with the processes and mechanisms we label, name (that is, nominate) and thereby define, categorize and 'box-off' **knowledge**. This often involves choices, politics and power issues concerning who, why and how this is taking place. For example, it might be that a very influential group of researchers**,** politicians, industrialists or philosophers, for various motives, steer or control **access** and discussion on an area through the labelling and representational processes they elect to employ. If a group of people are termed as, for example, 'troublemakers' or alternatively 'progressive radicals', either way, this 'labelling' or representational action begins to contribute to the formation of a reality. In turn, it will produce reactions in relation to the characterization that consequently emerges. For some people, the troublemakers may be a thorn in their side while, for others, the radical progressives may be a hopeful development. So, the creation of 'realities' through representation is a powerful act and we need to be mindful of the emergence of this in labelling and 'reality'-creating actions.

Ontologically**,** relativism and relativistic positions are quite different to realism and realistic positions. Relativism and relativistic approaches and traditions to ontology believe that reality is not absolute and that different individuals or groups of people may have various views of what constitutes reality. For example, **postmodern**

O

positions tend to espouse relativistic commitments that see reality and **meanings** as ever-changing, and ephemeral. In other words, here human beings *create* reality depending on what they believe it to be. In this manner, people and groups of people are seen to, in many ways, *socially construct* meanings in relation to the worlds and the things within it.

Critical realism offers something of a point situated in the continuum between realism and relativism (although we must tread cautiously here). It shows that impacts of social 'facts' or situations have very real consequences for human beings and the world. Vitally, in critical realism these situations exist whether or not we observe or engage with them, in that they have a reality external to the observer – that is, critical realism is not relativistic in this sense. However, at the same time it is keen to point up the role that human beings also play in *interpreting*, constructing, making sense and conceptualizing these situations (see **social constructionism** and **sense-making**).

KEY POINTS to reflect on in your research in relation to ontology:

- Do you think the 'realities' you research are a given; that is, already there? Alternatively, do you believe that 'reality' is made or constructed in some way? For example, do the ways people interact in a given situation or **context** *make* realities – for instance in the case of the commitments and actions of the followers of a religious faith?
- If you do believe that reality is fixed, solid, unchanging and something that is external to you that you straightforwardly observe and gather **data** on then you are likely to find a **deductive** (for example positivistic) style of methodological approach more fitting for your perception of the world.
- However, if you think that people, through interaction, create meanings about the world and that different **subjectivities** play a role in this then you are more likely to try to employ an **inductive** or **interpretive** style of **research methodology**. Therein the data are created and emerge from the field and you overtly acknowledge your subjective role.
- How and why do you come to believe that something is a 'fact' or the truth' or 'real'? The answer to this question will shape the types of methodological choices you make in order to obtain data. It will also have implications for the sorts of data you think might be observable and obtainable. And, how do you support or justify espoused or felt beliefs that you have about how 'facts' are established? What methods can be used to explore this?
- To what extent do you believe that reality is better understood in an *objective* (it is just there waiting to be observed and not an issue to be particularly considered) or *subjective* way (what is real and the meanings discerned from reality are made by *how people sense it* and its ontological status and meaning is not automatic, fixed or a given)?

Key Words
Being, Existence, Mainstream, Meaning, Normative, Objectivity, Positivism, Relativism, Social Constructionism, Solidity, Subjectivity

References
Bryman and Bell (2007); Fleetwood (2005); Jankowicz (2005); Linstead and Brewis (2007)

Open Question (*see* Closed Question)

O

Paradigm

A paradigm constitutes a model and its associated beliefs and values. In other words, a paradigm is, in effect, a conceptual and structural **representation** of a belief system, encompassing ideas and assumptions that will ultimately shape and reshape the way a person or persons see the world.

In conducting **research**, academics and **researchers** are often aligned with a particular paradigm and this conditions how they approach, conduct and produce research findings (Watson, 2006).

Strong adherence to particular paradigms can engender tensions and disagreements between differing academic viewpoints. A classic and long-running 'battle' has been between the natural scientific methodological approaches and social scientific approaches (see Denzin and Lincoln, 2008; Lincoln and Guba, 1985). Natural science or **experimental design** approaches tend to use approaches that subscribe to the use of **hypotheses** and techniques that prize **objectivity, representation, reductionism** and **deductivism**. Alternatively, social science approaches adopt methodological approaches, and paradigms that, to varying degrees, associate with **subjectivity**, **inductivism**, **reflexivity**, **sense-making** and **social constructionism**. A large number of social scientists find it improbable that research can be completely objective (see **objectivity**). They believe that there will always be some human subjective judgement at play. Social science perspectives suggest that if subjectivity is not considered to be in operation then there is a risk that some of the potential richness in the **data** and research situation will be lost.

Taking full account of paradigmatic tensions above, Kuhn (1970), among others, is one academic who has created controversy by describing the manner in which peer relationships and politics in scientific communities have a subjective role in the determination of the **knowledge** that goes on to become 'established science'. In contrast to this, commentators from the natural sciences frequently raise concerns regarding the assertions made by social scientists stating that the subjective nature of much of the work is flawed and problematic.

Within the literature of organization and management studies, Burrell and Morgan (1979) produced a suggested typology of research paradigms in the field. These are represented by one axis spanning objectivity (the organization is seen as real and we look at it as an external observer) on one side of the grid, with subjectivity (the organization is the result of human interaction and social constructionism – a result of the multiple, everyday long-term events and exchanges that create the place where people work) on the other end of this continuum. Then on the opposite side of the grid is the opposing axis with regulatory (the role of research is describe what happens in organizations) at one end of that continuum, and radical (the role of research is to prescribe what should happen in organizations) at the other. This is just one attempt, among many, to try to understand paradigms in organization and management. There are, and continue to be, extensive options and commentary in relation to paradigmatic choice (see also **critical realism**, **Critical Theory**, **deconstructionism, modernism, positivism**).

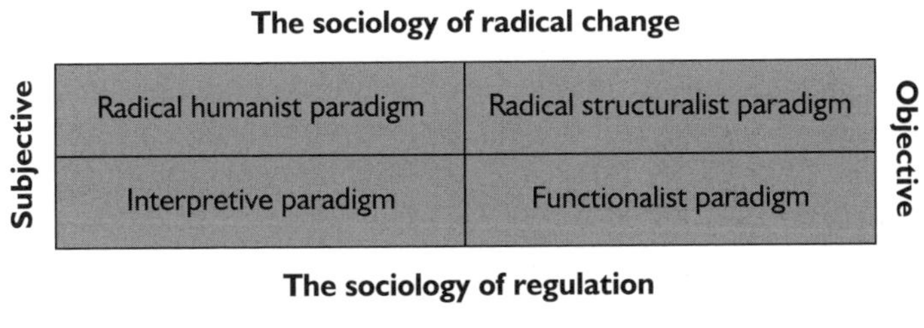

The sociology of radical change

| Subjective | Radical humanist paradigm | Radical structuralist paradigm | Objective |
| | Interpretive paradigm | Functionalist paradigm | |

The sociology of regulation

Figure 3 Burrell and Morgan's (1979) typology of research paradigms

Key Words
Critical Realism, Critical Theory, Data, Deconstructionism, Deductionism, Experimental Design, Hypotheses, Knowledge, Modernism, Objectivity, Positivism, Reductionism, Reflexivity, Representation, Sense-making, Social Constructionism, Subjectivity

References
Burrell and Morgan (1979); Denzin and Lincoln (2008); Kuhn (1970); Lincoln and Guba (1985); Watson (2006)

Participant Observation

Participant observation is a **research method** that comprises **data collection** via processes of watching and studying people in a given setting(s). **Researchers** using participant observation attempt to observe the routines, rituals, **language, discourse,** symbols and signs that people develop as they live, make sense (see **sense-making**) and **meaning** in the course of daily interactions. Waddington (2004) provides a succinct insight into participant observation. He details a continuum of participant observation situations that range from *complete observation* (where the researcher expressly separates him or herself from the **respondents** under observation) to, at the alternative end of the spectrum, *complete participant* (where the researcher conducting participant observation is totally immersed in the life of the social setting he or she is observing). He provides an excellent case study of his role in a strike at a brewery.

   Participant observation can embrace a range of methods embracing unstructured or semi-structured **interviews**. It usually forms part of an interpretivistic, ethnographic approach (see **interpretivism** and **ethnography**). In observing people, it is important to keep in mind the role of **reflexivity**, meaning the reciprocal interaction and exchanges between the researcher and the researched (that is, the research subjects or respondents). In other words, the researcher has a significant role in creating the research picture (see Wray-Bliss, 2004, and Wray-Bliss and Brewis, 2008, on this issue).

Key Words
Data Collection, Ethnography, Interpretivism, Language, Discourse, Meaning, Reflexivity, Sense-making

References
Allard-Poesi (2005); Waddington (2004); Wray-Bliss (2004); Wray-Bliss and Brewis (2008)

P

Phenomenology

Phenomenology is a philosophical position commonly associated with, among others, Husserl (1859–1938) and it focuses on the essences of any given experience. It is a rich and complex tradition that has grown to be seen as something of a counter position to **positivism** (see Bryman and Bell, 2007: 18–21 for a more detailed discussion).

In many **research methodology** texts, phenomenology has inappropriately come to be put into everyday usage as a generic synonym for **qualitative** methodologies or approaches using **inductivism** and **interpretivism**, This usage is best avoided and it is advisable to use a more specific term for the approach and methodology that is to be employed.

Key Words
Positivism, Qualitative, Research Methodology

References
Bryman and Bell (2007)

Pie Chart

A pie chart is a circular-shaped diagram that shows the relative size of a category of given **data**. This appears as a wedge in the pie. Pie charts are generally used to show the relative proportion of one category of data compared to another.

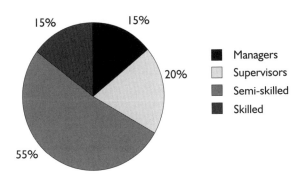

Figure 4 Relative size of types of employee in ABC Company plc workforce

A diagram such as a pie or **bar chart** can be useful for providing data in an alternative manner to text or tables and appeal to different aspects of learning style that different people possess. It is an all too common habit of some students to overload their **research** with multiple pie charts believing perhaps that this will impress or provide convincing information. In fact, too many charts can make the write-up look fragmented, under-narrated or explained and at times even childish. In general, this risks diminishing the potential valuable impact of diagram use. It is best to exercise good judgement when choosing to use diagrams.

Key Words
Data

References
Ha (2011); Payne (2011)

Pilot Study

A pilot study is a study that takes place before the main and actual study is undertaken. It is always shorter, smaller and faster than the main study. The purpose of the pilot study is to see if what you plan to do in the main study will work. The pilot study shows up potential problems and issues in the **research methods** and approaches and enables them to be modified before using them in the main study. This prevents the risk of potential waste of effort and resources by going straight into the main study with a poor **methodology** or methods.

It is important to run the pilot study a reasonable amount of time before the main study is to be conducted. This allows examination of any problems to do with, for example, the questions being asked, the potential **reliability** or **validity** of the **data** that might be obtained, the challenges of working in the field in order to secure the data and so on and so forth.

In one piece of illustrative research, a **researcher** went to a small manufacturing unit in the north of England with a structured **questionnaire** on worker values. A number of problems emerged only after the **research** was conducted, whereas, with a pilot study, these could have been avoided. Firstly, **access** to the workers during their work schedule had proved difficult. Secondly, the questions had not worked with the **respondents**, who did not recognize some of the terms of **language** as 'belonging to the way they saw the world' and the researcher was constantly explaining the questions, which interfered with the intended research process. Thirdly, it became apparent that something like a semi-structured **interview** or **focus group** might have worked more effectively. Based on unfavourable feedback from employees, the management were reluctant to allow the researcher to re-run the research differently: further access was declined and the opportunity lost.

P

Key Words
Access, Data, Methods, Methodology, Reliability, Respondents, Validity

References
Jankowicz (2005)

Population

When a piece of **research** is discussing **data** and it refers to the 'population' it means the entire number of the category, people, companies, **respondents** and so on that are present and exist in that grouping. It should not necessarily be seen as the same as or confused with the general use of population as used in demographics but the ideas are nevertheless related. The sample is the selection of a smaller group made from an overall population (see **sampling**). So, for example, if we wish to **interview** managers in a large multinational firm it may well not be possible to interview all of the thousands of managers who are employed there. The overall group of managers in this particular firm represents the 'population' for this given piece of research. It becomes apparent that there are too many and the cost in co-ordinating and booking interviews, of travelling to various locations is likely to be prohibitive. Therefore, it is sensible and appropriate, through some means, to identify a sample that will hopefully represent most of the views of the population.

Key Words
Data, Research, Sample

References
Saunders, Lewis and Thornhill (2007)

P

Positivism

The origins of positivism are strongly associated with the French writer Auguste Comte (1798–1857). Comte was dissatisfied with the conventional and traditional epistemological assumptions (see **epistemology**) underlying existing ways used to understand major social phenomena such as, for example, poverty, social class and population growth. He wanted to generate an approach that would introduce scientific techniques and principles to the study of social dimensions and, consequently, he is often cited as one of the founders of the modern discipline of sociology.

Certain epistemological values have come to be seen as underpinning positivistic approaches (Bryman and Bell, 2007) (see **epistemology**). These encompass:

- the employment of empirical observation to record **data**
- independence – from political constraints or interference
- the creation of **hypotheses** and the deduction of data in relation to these hypotheses
- a belief in **determinism** (that is, cause and effect)
- a willingness to undertake **reductionism** and generalization
- the possibility of cross-analysis between different groups and entities

(See **empiricism** and **deductivism**.)

If, for example, a **researcher** is electing to adopt a positivistic approach in his or her **research**, he or she is likely to do all that is possible to follow a logical experiment-like process and employ **deductive** reasoning. At the same time, he or she will be seeking to maintain the **objectivity** of the research by trying to stop what might be viewed by others as **subjective** opinions and assumptions from impacting on the study. Positivism is just one methodological **paradigm** among many.

Key Words
Deductivism, Experimentation, Hypothesis, Objectivity, Reductionism

References
Bryman and Bell (2007); Clegg, Kornberger and Pitsis (2011)

Postmodernism

Postmodernism is a highly sophisticated and multidimensional philosophy. It tends to view experiences and phenomena as fragmented, emergent, fleeting, and ever-changing and engages signs, symbols, **language** and **discourse** to attempt **representation** of these things. **Research methodologies** that employ postmodern-style methodologies tend to offer relativistic arguments that are reluctant to say definitely 'what is' or 'is not' (see **research**

methodology and **relativism**). Rather the research findings tend to constitute various impressions regarding what may be possible to say at a given point of time and from a particular point of view. In summary, it can be seen that 'reality' and the possibility of definitively saying what 'is the case' or not in a piece of research influenced by postmodernism becomes something of a slippery and difficult task to grasp.

Postmodernism, for example, stands in contrast to the stable and fixed ways that the world is presented through **modernism** and **rationalism**. It has evolved, transformed and even, in some ways, is incorporated into, or appropriated by modernism and modernistic practices in organizations (Dereli and Stokes, 2007). In terms of **ontology** and **epistemology**, whereas modernism and its kindred **positivism** and **deductivism** value **objectivity**, linear appreciations of research, postmodernism generally adopts ways of making sense of situations and contexts that embrace **subjectivity**, and emergent **sense-making**. For illustrations of the use of postmodernistic approaches to research phenomena and subjects, it is useful to look over materials in what is termed the now broad area of **critical management studies** or critical management.

Key Words
Language, Modernism, Objectivity, Ontology, Rationalism, Relativism, Representation, Sense-making, Subjectivity

References
Allard-Poesi (2005); Dereli and Stokes (2007); Thompson (1993)

Poststructuralism (*also* Post-structuralism)

P

Poststructuralism emerged primarily in France in the 1960s and is aligned with a number of French philosophers including Deleuze (1925–1995), Kristeva (1941–), Foucault (1926–1984) and Derrida (1930–2004). The central characteristics of poststructuralism indicate the manner in which **language** produces 'reality'. It is especially concerned with the way in which human language, emotion and sensory perceptions create feelings and behaviour.

In terms of **research methodology**, much of what can be said regarding postmodern (see **postmodernism**) approaches is potentially pertinent to poststructuralist approaches. Postructuralism provides an important critical analytical approach with which to critique mainstream positivistic and deductivist management (see **positivism** and **deductivism**). Nevertheless, such critiques also point up concerns as to the limits of how far language can portray reality. If language-created reality becomes so idiosyncratic then it is difficult to see how it might be possible to develop a generalized sense of firm, useable findings and recommendations that practitioners can use. Moreover, to concentrate on language means that **researchers** need to make 'truth' claims regarding what language might mean, whereas interpretively (see **interpretivism**), it might be more suitable to ask **respondents** what they aim to say. Thus, poststructuralism, similarly to **postmodernism**, has, by its essential ideological characteristics, proved a difficult domain around which to develop and maintain clearly outlined positions. This is no surprise given the fluid nature of the **concepts** underpinning it. **Discourse, hermeneutics** or **content analysis** are typical approaches that might employ poststructuralist (or postmodernist) methodologies (Allan, 2010; Willis, 2007).

Key Words
Deductivism, Discourse, Interpretivism, Language, Postmodernism, Representation, Subjectivity

References
Allan (2010); Contu, Driver and Jones (2010); Knights (2002); Willis (2007)

Primary Data (*see* **Data**)

P

Qualitative

Qualitative is a generic term used in a range of **contexts** including, for example, qualitative **research**, qualitative **methods**, qualitative **data**, qualitative **analysis** and so on and so forth. It is difficult to provide a definitive and categorical outline of all the **meanings** that could be invoked in relation to this term but generally it is considered to include, by way of illustration, approaches that embrace **subjectivity, constructionism, textual analysis, ethnography, hermeneutics, phenomenology, postmodernism, poststructuralism, deconstructionism** and **discourse analysis.**

(See also the entries on **data, research methods**, and **research methodology**.)

Key Words
Analysis, Constructionism, Contexts, Data, Deconstructionism, Discourse Analysis, Ethnography, Hermeneutics, Method, Methodology, Phenomenology, Postmodernism, Poststructuralism Subjectivity, Textual Analysis

References
Eriksson and Kovalainen (2008); Silverman (2006, 2010a,b)

Quantitative

The term *quantitative* usually means the use of some form of numbers of **statistics** to portray, analyse and draw conclusions on **data**. Although not exclusively (for example see the entries on **data, research methods** and **research methodology**), this is conducted with methodologies rooted in **deductivism** and **positivism** (Donaldson, 1996, 2005; Ha, 2011; Kremelberg, 2011).

Key Words
Data, Deductivism, Positivism, Research Methods, Research Methodology, Statistics

References
Donaldson (1996, 2005); Ha (2011); Kremelberg (2011)

Questionnaires

A questionnaire is essentially a collection of questions on a particular topic. This is usually drawn up by the **researcher(s)** and the questions should be carefully phrased and laid out in an appropriate order so as to illicit useful and meaningful **data** from targeted **respondents**. It is possible to conduct questionnaires in a range of ways including face to face, post, email or fax.

Typically, questionnaires will be structured, semi-structured or unstructured. A structured questionnaire details all the questions and will probably contain a range of 'yes/no' type **closed questions**. A semi-structured questionnaire will contain some key 'signposting' **open questions** that indicate and direct the general flow of the discussion but allow free-ranging comments by the respondents. An unstructured questionnaire is unusual but generally would allow the respondents to write freely in relation to a topic. The latter two types of questionnaire are likely, although not necessarily, to involve the researcher asking the questions. Structured and semi-structured forms tend to be the most commonly used.

The oft-cited advantages of using a questionnaire include potential cost-effectiveness and possible high degree of accurate information whereas the potential disadvantages include poor questionnaire design leading to poor data collected and effects such as 'tick box syndrome' where respondents 'pay lip service' to completing it.

When students come to do a piece of **research**, more often than not, they immediately decide to do a questionnaire. This is because they feel comfortable and familiar with this approach having encountered it numerous times in their everyday life. Moreover, other research instrument alternatives may appear more complex and difficult to develop. There is a cautionary note here. It is very easy to draw up a poor quality questionnaire but a good questionnaire that is fit for purpose and achieves the **data collection** it desires requires considerably more preparation. Many **research methodology** books contain commentaries on questions (see a useful exposition

Q

in Wilson, 2010: 148–58). Also remember that it is useful looking under the social sciences in general and other specific fields such as marketing research. These often have a wide range of materials that can be applied to, and adopted for, business, management and organization research purposes.

Key Words
Closed Question, Data, Data Collection, Open Question, Respondents

References
Behling and Law (2000); Remler and Van Ryzin (2011)

Q

Rationalism

Rationalism is a belief that is underpinned by principles of **causality**, **determinism**, **linear** logic and **objectivity**. It supersedes and challenges pre-modernistic thinking of the Ancient World. Rationalism is an integral plank of the philosophies of **modernism** and **positivism** (see **research** discussions in Casey, 2004; Di Maggio and Powell, 2002).

Key Words
Causality, Determinism, Linear, Modernism, Objectivity, Positivism

References
Casey (2004); Di Maggio and Powell (2002)

Realism

Realism involves discussion on issues of existence and being. Issues of reality pertain to an area of philosophy called **ontology**. Ontology is a field that is concerned with exploring the nature of reality, that is, what reality *is* or *might be*.

For approaches such as **deductivism** and **positivism**, 'reality' is generally taken at face value. In other words, a 'fact' is a fact (that is, not constructed or imagined into being and action as is the case with, for example, **constructionism**). Moreover, in relation to this, objects and artefacts are considered to exist independently of the observer's gaze – they are still present, and in the same state, when he or she is not looking. **Rationalism** is an important **concept** in association with the notions of reality.

The above ideas contrast with, for example, **inductivism, interpretivism, postmodernism, poststructuralism, Critical Theory** and **critical realism** which see, to varying degrees, a central constructivist role for **respondents** to 'make' their reality through **discourse**, **language** and **symbols**.

Key Words
Constructionism, Critical Theory, Critical Realism, Inductivism, Interpretivism, Ontology, Positivism, Postmodernism, Poststructuralism, Rationalism

References
Ackroyd and Fleetwood (2001); Woźniak (2010)

Reductionism

Reductionism involves processes of breaking down, classifying, categorizing or, in essence, reducing issues, objects, situations and environments to the elements that they appear composed of. Reductionism is a central principle of **rationalism, deductivism** and **positivism.**

Critics of reductionism claim that it involves oversimplification of complex environments and experiences. Hence, more inductive and interpretivistic approaches generally seek to avoid reductionism (see **inductivism** and **interpretivism**).

Key Words
Categories, Classifications, Deductivism, Inductivism, Interpretivism, Positivism, Rationalism

References
Al-Amoudi (2007); Fairhurst (2004)

Referencing

Referencing is the term given to the act and process of indicating sources of materials and ideas in a text. There are a number of different systems of referencing to choose from including, for example, Harvard, Vancouver and APA. Each system has its own format and style rules on how to lay out References.

R

Basic examples of Harvard, Vancouver and APA referencing are provided as an indication below:

Harvard Referencing Format – Single Authored Book and Article
Dupont, J. (2011) *Business Today*, London, Queen Publishing House.
Dupont, J. (2011) 'An analysis of organizational learning – new perspectives', *The Journal of Business*, 13(2): pp. 233–54.

Vancouver Referencing Format – Single Authored Book and Article
Dupont, J. *Business Today.* London: Queen Publishing House; 2011.
Dupont, J. An analysis of organizational learning – new perspectives. *The Journal of Business* 2011; 13(2): 233–54.

APA Referencing Format – Single Authored Book and Article
Dupont, J. (2011). *Business Today*. London: Queen Publishing House.
Dupont, J. (2011). An analysis of organizational learning – new perspectives. *The Journal of Business*, 13(2): 233–54.

Each of these systems is considerably more complex and extensive than these brief illustrations can provide. It is usually the case that a given university or institute will have support materials or guidelines on the particular system that it expects students' work to adopt. There are many guides available, particularly on the internet. Useful current examples can be found at a range of university library and learning resources sites. It is worthwhile to examine the following sites for further details:

• http://libweb.anglia.ac.uk on Harvard Referencing
• http://www.soton.ac.uk/library/resources on Vancouver Referencing
• http://ilrb.cf.ac.uk/citing References/apatutorial on APA Referencing

These particular examples will of course be prone to update and change: however, many comparable resources can be readily located via the internet.

One of the reasons it is important to reference is that it provides due recognition to the original author of the text. A further reason is that it enables a reader of a text to better follow the argument. By knowing the sources and writers that are influencing somebody who has produced a text we can in essence 'see where he or she is coming from' in the formulation of their own ideas. Finally, referencing is an important safeguard for a student against being charged with plagiarism, copying or cheating.

Key Words
Argument, Plagiarism

References
Fisher (2010); Wilson (2010)

Reflexivity

Reflexivity involves the way in which the **researcher** and the **research** participants interact with each other during the course of a given research project. In a symbiotic and reciprocal manner, the researcher and the research **respondents** are likely to experience, and be affected by, the process of the research and this is turn affects the **data** and the findings. For example, in a research project the researcher may be involved in studying and questioning research respondents or participants using, for instance, **participant observation**. Many would argue that the respondents are inevitably and irreversibly affected by having met and known the researcher: that is, once he or she has entered the lives of the researched through the project, his or her impact and the memory of him or her plays a role in the respondents' lives – they co-create each other. Equally, the respondents or research participants are likely to have a similar impact on the researcher.

Deductive, positivistic-style approaches to methodology seek to control and limit the impacts of reflexivity by separating the researchers' subjective opinions from findings produced from data (see **deductivism**, **positivism** and **subjectivity**). In this way, it is believed that **bias** is decreased or eradicated from the findings and their **validity** enhanced. In contrast, inductive, interpretivistic approaches are more likely to acknowledge and embrace the role of reflexivity and to take account of the subjective ways themes emerge from the data provided by the respondents and the researchers' perception of them (see **inductivism**, **interpretivism** and **subjectivity**).

Key Words
Inductivism, Interpretivism, Subjectivity, Voice

References
Alvesson and Sköldberg (2009); Rhodes and Brown (2005); Waddington (2004); Wray-Bliss and Brewis (2008)

Relativism

R

Relativism is a **concept** associated with **ontology.** Relativism suggests that universal statements of 'fact' and 'truth' are not tenable or sustainable. In contrast, relativism proposes that what 'is' or 'is not' in the world in any given setting is likely to be the consequence of a **language**, **discourse** perspective, operating in a more constructivist-like manner in specific, rather than **generalizable**, **contexts** (see also **realism, ontology** and **constructionism**).

Relativism is closely associated with approaches such as **postmodernism** and **poststructuralism**: however, it is rejected by approaches such as **positivism**. Relativism is often contrasted with absolutism, which is a belief in categorical and universal statements on matters and phenomena (see Van Maanen, 2010; also see a wide range of useful articles in *Cultural Studies – Critical Methodologies*).

Key Words
Discourse, Language, Ontology, Postmodernism, Poststructuralism

References
Van Maanen (2010)

Reliability

In a research **context**, reliability is a measure applied to all **research** and its intent is to assess the degree to which the **data collection** and **analysis** would be approximately similar if the work were to be repeated by the **researcher** or another researcher. In other words, if the piece of research was done again, whether by the same researcher or not, to what extent would it be likely to produce the same results. It is also a question of 'Can this work be done again?' or 'Is it repeatable?' This is an important assessment because it shows that the **methodology** and **method** of the research project are not constructed in a manner that is wholly based on some personal dimension of the researcher or research project.

The researcher, through explanations and descriptions of processes, structures and techniques employed in the research, needs to be able to demonstrate that repeatability in some shape or form is possible. (This topic is covered to some extent in many **research methods** texts: see Maylor and Blackmon, 2005: 157–9 for a useful overview.)

Key Words
Analysis, Data Collection, Method, Methodology, Researcher

References
Maylor and Blackmon (2005)

Representation

Representation is the process of categorizing, classifying and labelling the world. It is a process which is very much part of deductivistic, rationalistic, positivistic and modernistic ways of approaching **epistemology** and **ontology** (see **deductivism, epistemology, modernism, ontology, positivism, rationalism**). Critical and inductive approaches generally see representation as problematic (see **inductivism** and **interpretivism**). They generally see **meaning** and **knowledge** as being more complex and rich and not readily delineated, or classified in such categorical manners (see Ellis, 2008; Mescher, Benschop and Doorewaard, 2010).

Key Words
Deductivism, Epistemology, Inductivism, Interpretivism, Modernism, Ontology, Positivism, Rationalism

References
Ellis (2008); Mescher, Benschop and Doorewaard (2010)

Research

According to Collis and Hussey's (2009: 1) definition, research is:

- a process of enquiry and investigation
- systematic and methodical, and
- increases knowledge.

As a process, research generally follows the stages of defining, designing, doing and describing (adapted from Maylor and Blackmon, 2005).

Undertaking research is a process that will involve many choices and decisions with regard to various **research methods** and **methodologies** and their appropriateness for the project in hand. An important thought to consider is your view on the possibility or desirability of **objectivity** or the role of **subjectivity** in the research. For many students, there is a prima facie or initial assumption that research is, and should always be, objective. However, inductive and deductive approaches have contrasting ideological commitments (see **inductivism** and **deductivism**). To some degree such choices could even be considered to have political dimension (with a small 'p', to use the colloquialism). How we see the world and believe that facts and truths are established often indicates a great deal regarding underlying values and beliefs.

R

Key Words
Methods, Methodology, Objectivity, Subjectivity

References
Collis and Hussey (2009); Maylor and Blackmon (2005)

Research Design

The research design phase of a piece of **research** involves making decisions regarding what particular or specific topic is to be examined. **Research questions** then need to be developed and subsequently the **researcher** needs to decide what **methods** and methodologies and theories will be appropriate to deal with these questions (see **research methodology** and **theory**). In turn, **access** and **data collection** will need to be organized and when the **data** have been collected, decisions will need to taken with regard to the planning, **writing up** and presentation of the research findings (see Eriksson and Kovalainen, 2008; Polonsky and Waller, 2011).

In summary, it can be seen that the research 'journey', with all its potential twists and turns, needs to be planned out as clearly and in as much detail as possible. This does not mean that adjustments or changes will not be necessary but, at the very least, some form of guide and contingency can be envisaged (Maylor and Blackmon, 2005: 154–62 offer some useful insights in this regard).

Key Words
Access, Data Collection, Methods, Methodology, Research Questions, Theory, Writing Up

References
Eriksson and Kovalainen (2008); Polonsky and Waller (2011)

Research Method

In general terms, a research method is a manner or a way of doing things. The use of the term *method* implies that it is likely to involve a particular system or procedure.

Within various fields of **research methodologies** a wide and varied range of research methods are possible. It is important to reiterate and elaborate this point in the form of an illustration as it is often a source of potential confusion for students. It is common for students to start their thinking on the **research** project or **dissertation** by thinking which research methods they would like to use. The reason for students feeling comfortable with using methods (rather than methodologies) as a starting point is because methods seem to have a solid aspect to them. They involve the student *doing* something, taking physical action with them as in the case, for example, of posting out or completing a **questionnaire** or drafting and conducting an **interview**. In this way, although they involve intellectual processes, research methods have very evident experiential aspects.

Research methodologies are somewhat different from research methods in that, while they may well shape action and the structure of a piece of research, they are as much about the way of the **researcher's** thinking or 'being' in relation to that piece of research. This is expressed through the **epistemology** and **ontology** of the chosen research methodology. Thus, research methodologies are more about the spirit and belief system in which the research will be carried out. For this reason, students sometimes find the idea of needing to identify and espouse a particular research methodology more difficult than choosing research methods. To summarize in a simple metaphor, research methods can be likened to a craft person's tools but research methodologies point at the beliefs, values and traditions he or she holds that underpin and overarch the craft and influence the way the tools are held and employed.

The above insight is illustrated in the diagram below which shows that research methods are shaped by the methodology within which they are used. For example, the way in which questionnaires are designed, employed and analysed will be very dependent on whether or not an inductive or deductive style research approach is being engaged (see **inductivism** and **deductivism**). An interview or questionnaire used within an inductive methodology is likely to aim to gather rich **data** which will provide the **sense-making** and social constructive process that **respondents** use (see **social constructionism**). Equally, the design of the interview or questionnaire will allow the researcher to conduct analyses with notions of **subjectivity** and **reflexivity** in mind. Alternatively, a more deductive, positivistic research methodological approach will aim to use structured interviews and questionnaires (with more **closed**-style **questions**) in order to gather data that can be used to test and verify predetermined **variables** and **hypotheses** with **objectivity** (Aguinas, Pierce, Bosco and Muslin, 2008; Buchanan and Bryman, 2007; Spector and Brannich, 2010).

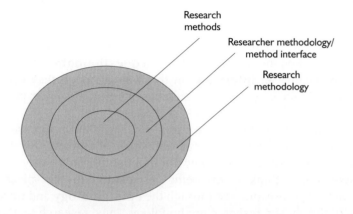

Figure 5 The Relationship of: Researcher – Research methods – Research methodologies

There is a plethora of material available on research methods in electronic, internet and paper-based sources. Among the vast array of materials it is worth looking at, for example, *Organizational Research Methods; Journal of Mixed Methods Research.*

Key Words
Deductivism, Inductivism, Objectivity, Research Methodology, Reflexivity, Subjectivity

References
Aguinas, Pierce, Bosco and Muslin (2008); Buchanan and Bryman (2007); Spector and Brannich (2010)

Research Methodology

Research methodology concerns the philosophy, approach and general **frame of reference** you will use to study, analyse and understand the research field and phenomena that you are interested in.

Research methodology will usually involve choosing from a range of well-established positions. Commonly employed approaches include, for example, **positivism** and **interpretivism.**

Different research methodologies will usually be underpinned by characteristics based on differing degrees of either **subjectivity** and **inductivism** or, alternatively, **objectivity** and **deductivism**. It is important to remain aware of this because as you progress through the various phases of your research study (for example **research proposal**, fieldwork, **analysis** and **writing up**), it is not possible to switch between these values and positions. A common instance of this problem is when students claim that they are following, for example, **interpretivism** as their approach and then begin to talk about 'trying to avoid **bias**'. This is inherently impossible and problematic in a methodology that so clearly espouses the role of subjectivity in the research setting.

Although reference was made to **positivism** and **interpretivism** above, there are clearly a wide range of methodological and philosophical approaches that have been developed over the centuries. These include, by merely way of illustration: **deconstruction**, **postmodernism**, **poststructuralism**, post-postivism, **Grounded Theory**, **Critical Theory** and **critical realism.** This brief indicative list underlines that there are plainly more choices than the two that students usually learn about. (At this juncture, it is also important to underscore the concerns about the use of the term **phenomenology** which were addressed under that entry heading.)

Remember that your choice of a particular methodology should not be an arbitrary thing, rather, it should match your own political, sociological and psychological views and commitments. In other, words, it should tally with the way you see and perceive the world – your **Weltanschauung**. We use a methodology because it fits with the way we typically make sense of the world (see **sense-making**). Whatever your choice in relation to methodology, it is important to read around your approach in a range of research textbooks. Moreover, find articles that have used your approach (something students often omit to do) and see how your choice of methodology is handled in the paper.

R

Key Words
Deductivism, Inductivism, Interpretivism, Objectivity, Postivism, Subjectivity

References
Bryman and Bell (2007); Eriksson and Kovalainen (2008); Fisher (2010); Wilson (2010)

Research Proposal

A research proposal is like a detailed plan for a piece of research (see **research design**). Although a number of formats are possible, the format will generally comprise the following sections:

Title *(of the proposed research project)*

Introduction

*Research **Aims** and **Objectives***
  (**Research questions** may sometimes be introduced here, especially if the work is adopting a positivistic, deductivistic approach: see **positivism, deductivism**.)

Literature Review
  (This will be a review of the articles, books and materials relevant to the terms employed in research title, aims and objectives and, perhaps, questions.
  It should be noted that, sometimes, research questions may be indicated here stemming from the review or, alternatively, as indicated they may be established at the outset.)

Research Methodology

Access *Issues*

Ethical Considerations
(see **Ethics**)

***Data Collection** Approaches*

*Data **Analysis** Approaches*

***Writing Up** Approach*

It is an excellent idea to get feedback from an expert on the ideas in your proposal. This will give you the opportunity to modify it so as to ensure it is successful. A proposal might also be written in close conjunction with a **pilot study** which allows a **researcher** to actually test his or her approaches in the field and to eradicate any potential difficulties (see Cameron and Price, 2009: 262–81 for a useful overview).

Key Words
Access, Aims, Analysis, Data Collection, Ethics, Introduction, Literature Review, Objectives, Pilot Study, Researcher, Research Questions, Title, Writing Up

References
Cameron and Price (2009)

Research Question(s)

Questions are words and phrases that express a desire to find out some **data** or information. Research questions are interrogative statements that aim to find out points regarding a specific topic or subject. Jankowicz (2005: 38–45) offers some useful ideas on research questions as concerning 'what are you really trying to do?' and 'what is it that is most useful to do?' In turn, Fisher (2010: 34–9) suggests useful tactics and techniques including, for example, using post-its to map out ideas on a desk or wall.

As is the case with the **title**, **aims** and **objectives**, the research questions should be shaped to deal with something that is of interest to you. You will be spending a considerable amount of time engaged with the project so it would be better if it is something that will stimulate you.

Key Words
Aims, Objectives, Title

References
Fisher (2010); Jankowicz (2005)

Researcher

A researcher is a person who is using a particular approach, technique and methodology to find out information and **knowledge** regarding a particular and specific topic. Jankowicz (2005) offers a useful chapter on 'Research Roles' which covers a wide range of issues relating to identity, approach and behaviour of researchers. The identity of researchers and the **respondents** with which they engage and develop relationships provokes comment in most textbooks and a wide range of academic articles. The moment a student gathers ideas for an assignment or undertakes a **dissertation** or **thesis**, he or she becomes a researcher.

R

Key Words
Knowledge, Respondents

References
Jankowicz (2005)

Respondent

A respondent is a person who participates in a piece of **research**. The word 'participant' is synonym for respondent. There are key ethical issues in relation to respondents (see **ethics**). Above all, it is imperative that the respondent does not experience any harm, in any way whatsoever, as a consequence of the research either at the time it is conducted or subsequently. **Access** is something that commonly needs to be negotiated and agreed with respondents.

Depending on the **research methodology** adopted by the **researcher**, there may be little or intensive contact and experiences shared with respondents. For example, at one end of a spectrum, the research may consist of a **closed question** postal **questionnaire** that involves little or no contact. At the other end, the **researcher** may be engaged in intensive **participant observation**, sharing many aspects of the respondents' lives. There is an extensive literature on respondents (see, by way of illustration, Dundon and Ryan, 2010; Kolar and Kolar, 2008; and Nichols and Hunter-Childs, 2009).

Key Words

Access, Ethics, Participant Observation, Research Methodology, Researcher

References

Dundon and Ryan (2010); Kolar and Kolar (2008); Nichols and Hunter-Childs (2009)

R

S s

Sampling

Sampling involves using various techniques to select a part of the overall **population** of a given domain or sphere. For example, if a company has 120 employees then this is effectively the 'population' of all the people in the company. If, therefore, a **researcher** decides to interview 20 employees then this would be a sample selected from within that overall population. The way in which sampling is to be approached will depend on a number of factors. These include, for example, the **research methodology** and **methods** to be employed.

It is not uncommon for the researcher to produce a sampling frame that will aim to encompass a collection of respondents who, or subject targets that, will provide a representative group of the overall population. This may well involve some form of, by way of illustration, stratified or cluster sampling. Stratified sampling involves dividing up the **research** field or notional population into clearly delineated and categorized strata, such as by age, class, geographical location, or job type. Of course, some of these might be already established or widely recognized. The task then is to identify a sample that proportionally reflects the numbers of **respondents** or subjects in each layer of the target organization or setting. Some of the **objectives** of this process include establishing and reinforcing the **validity**, **reliability** and **generalizability** of the subsequent research.

On the other hand, cluster sampling involves identifying particular locations or situations of relevance to the research (for example specific streets, social groups or industrial estates) and then targeting respondents who have a connection or relevance to those cluster points. For positivistic approaches, this process is a central part of ensuring that the reliability, validity and **objectivity** of the student can be assured (see **positivism**). It is likely that a technique based on **statistics** may be employed. Of course, these are also important considerations for inductive, interpretivistic methodologies, although here samples are often smaller and more localized and are not intended to suggest any broad claims to representativeness or generalizability (see **inductivism** and **interpretivism**). The approach you take to sampling will depend on the philosophical, epistemological and ontological commitments of the methodology you are using (see **epistemology** and **ontology**). In brief, other forms of sampling include:

- *Random sampling* – Each member of a given population has an equal chance of being chosen.
- *Systematic sampling* – This is semi-random sampling: a sampling frame is established and a point randomly chosen within it. From this point onwards items are chosen at regular intervals.
- *Quota sampling* – This is where the researcher has been given quotas within a sampling frame and he or she attempts to fill the quota level that has been allocated.
- *Convenience sampling* – This is a commonly used method by students. It tends to build a sample from people and points that are readily available to the researcher (that is, to which he or she has **access**). One of the issues of convenience sampling is that the researcher is likely to draw on friends, family and people associated with these groups. This can mean that the **data** collected actually come from a fairly narrow band of the possible population. This can have limiting implications for validity and generalizability.

There is a substantial commentary in a range of textbooks on sampling as well as a broad and rich journal literature (see the following merely by way of indicative illustrations: Abrams, 2010; Draucker, Martsoff, Ross and Rusk, 2007; Saunders, Lewis and Thornhill, 2007).

Many students automatically state that they are going to do random sampling because this is the usual practice and it is expected of them. However, when they begin to discuss their sampling approach it often transpires that it is some other form of sampling. Useful random sampling, for purposes of validity, reliability and generalizability, is actually very challenging and requires extensive resources.

Key Words

Generalizability, Methods, Population, Reliability, Research Methodology, Statistics, Validity

References

Abrams (2010); Draucker, Martsoff, Ross and Rusk (2007); Saunders, Lewis and Thornhill (2007)

Secondary Data (*see* Data)

Semiotics

Semiotic(s) means the significance and **meaning** of signs and symbols particularly in relation to communication and **language.** Semiotics is often debated in relation to **discourse analysis**. Although not exclusively, methodological approaches such as **postmodernism, poststructuralism, inductivism** and **ethnography** often find great analytical depth and value in semiotic analyses.

Key Words
Inductivism, Language, Meaning, Postmodernism, Poststructuralism

References
Hancock (2005); Rosenthal and Peccei (2006)

Sense-making

People generate understanding of the world through a range of ways including: **discourse, semiotics,** personal histories, **meaning.** In the social sciences in recent decades, the **concept** of sense-making has attracted increasing attention. Among a range of commentators, Karl Weick (1995, 2001) has been a seminal influence.

Sense-making involves individuals looking at the **contexts** and environments around them in order to see how they link to earlier experiences. Storytelling and narratives are commonplace in this process (see **narrative research)**. Weick suggests that there are a number of characteristics typically involved in processes of sense-making:

- *Ongoing* – we never stop making sense.
- *Retrospective* – we look backwards over the past to be able to understand.
- *Plausible* – sense-making is never perfect; it is makeshift and ongoing just for the purposes of temporary understanding.
- *Images* are made full use of when we sense-make – we make sketches, draw pictures with our hands, and generally try to represent things (see **representation**).

S

- *Rationalize* – we use logic and we simplify to be able to comprehend (see **rationalism**).
- *People,* not things, undertake sense-making.
- *Doing* and talking help us to provide the 'raw materials' to work through what we are trying to understand.

Key Words
Contexts, Discourse, Meaning, Narrative Research, Rationalism, Semiotics, Storytelling

References
Allard-Poesi (2005); Weick (1995, 2001)

Skew (*see* Normal Distribution)

Social Constructionism (*see* Constructionism)

Statistics

Statistics comprises a series of numeric and mathematical techniques that can be used to compute and analyse **data**. Statistics, as numerical data, are engaged in both the social and natural sciences, although the latter is particularly oriented towards their use. The characteristics of deductive **research** of **objectivity**, **reductionism** and **causality** lend themselves well to statistics (see **deductivism**). A range of techniques are typically employed including, for example, **correlation**, **linear regression**, **chi square test** and regression **analysis.**

Key Words
Causality, Deductivism, Objectivity, Reductionism

References
Ha (2011); Payne (2011)

Storytelling (*see* Narrative Research)

Subjectivity

Subjectivity relates to points of, and opinions derived from, individual or group collectives' perspectives and experiences. Subjectivity is recognized and acknowledged as an important aspect of naturalistic field approaches such as **ethnography**, **inductivism** and **interpretivism**. These approaches are naturalistic in the sense that they desire to glean and collect **data** from settings as they actually occur and in their full and usual **context**. These methodologies believe that **researchers** play a role in developing the data. This takes place when they are interacting with **respondents** in the field and also when they are **interpreting**, analysing data and findings and ultimately, writing up.

For other methodological perspectives, however, the idea of subjectivity is generally considered to be problematic. This is particularly the case in deductive, modernistic, positivistic and rationalistic approaches (see, **deductivism, modernism, positivism** and **rationalism**). For these perspectives, any possibility of subjective interference or 'contamination' of data is seen as a denigration of the **objectivity** of the **research** and this could have detrimental effects on **validity** and **reliability** (see Bergström and Knights, 2006, and Böhm and Batta, 2010 for illustrations of consideration of subjectivity in research).

Key Words
Context, Deductivism, Ethnography, Inductivism, Interpretivism, Modernism, Objectivity, Positivism, Rationalism, Reliability, Validity

References
Bergström and Knights (2006); Böhm and Batta (2010)

Survey Research

A survey is a **research** approach that involves asking questions of a group of people. Often it is used to cover a very large number of people or sites although smaller-scale surveys are possible. The purpose of using a survey is often to catch a range of facts or attitudes or information on behaviours.

Within a survey, a number of **research methods** or, as the expression is sometimes used, *survey instruments*, can be employed included **interviews** or different types of **questionnaire**. For larger-scale surveys, the cost and availability of resources may be an issue. If there are not many **researchers** then, for example, face-to-face interviews will not be feasible. In this particular instance, postal or email self-administered questionnaires may be more practical.

In designing the survey instrument all the usual issues regarding phrasing questions in the most effective manner, developing a **sampling** frame and running a **pilot study** for the survey should be considered (Fink, 2009; Fowler, 2008; Maylor and Blackmon, 2005: 182–99).

Key Words
Interview, Questionnaire, Research Method

References
Fink (2009); Fowler (2008); Maylor and Blackmon (2005)

Symbolic Interactionism

This is a philosophical and **research** methodological tradition that suggests that our own self-awareness and **identity** is a consequence of our multiple and repeated interactions with others (see **research methodology**). Reciprocally, people behave towards things and people in relation to the **meaning** these things have for them. Symbolic interactionism has been an important movement in sociological thought and is particularly associated with George Herbert Mead (1863–1931) and Herbert Blumer (1900–1987). While it is not necessarily often overtly mentioned in many business, management and organization texts or papers, it is nevertheless an underlying influence for primarily, although not exclusively, inductive-style research approaches (see **inductivism**) (see, by way of example, Armstrong, 1999; LoConto and Jones-Pruett, 2006; Lundgren, 2005).

Key Words
Inductivism, Research Methodology

References
Armstrong (1999); LoConto and Jones-Pruett (2006); Lundgren (2005)

Textual Analysis (*see* Analysis, Discourse Analysis, Hermeneutics, Inductivism, Interpretivism, Language, Semiotics)

Thematic Analysis

Thematic analysis is the process of looking over **data** in order to identify recurrent, salient and self-evident points, issues, words, terms, events, **language**, **discourse**, images, allusions and so on and so forth. These noticeably repetitive pieces of data can be clustered together under a label (that may also emerge from the **respondent** data or be allocated by the **researcher**) for the theme.

Thematic analysis is a technique that is used in a range of research methodologies (see **research methodology**). It tends to be particularly employed in inductive and interpretivistic-style **research** (see **inductivism** and **interpretivism**). In these sorts of approaches, researchers often read and re-read the data several times in order to code and identify prevailing themes (see **coding**). This approach is also termed **constant comparison**. One particular approach that employs specific schemes of coding themes is **Grounded Theory**, although this is not the only process available.

As the themes emerge from the **analysis** they can be assembled into a conceptual framework that begins to point at the development of emergent theory.

Key Words
Analysis, Coding, Data, Grounded Theory, Inductivism, Interpretivism, Research Methodology, Researcher, Respondent

References
Eriksson and Kovalainen (2008)

Theory

A theory is an attempt to construct an explanation of a system or collection of ideas on particular issues or problems. Theories are produced and reside within and across a wide range of methodological and philosophical perspectives (see **research methodology**). There are myriad theories at large in the world. Each theory has its own ontological and epistemological roots (see **epistemology** and **ontology**). In basic terms, a theory is simply a scheme or framework that seeks to understand how something relates to something else, operates or functions in relation to other things, people or phenomena.

Key Words
Epistemology, Ontology, Research Methodology

References
Clegg, Kornberger and Pitsis (2011)

Thesis

A thesis is the written text and document produced and submitted to be considered for a doctoral award. Depending on the degree being taken, if successful, this might result in a number of named awards being made including, among others, Doctor of Philosophy (PhD), Doctor of Education (DEd or EdD), Doctor of Business Administration (DBA) (Dunleavy, 2003; Murray, 2006).

In contrast to doctorates, degrees such as Bachelor's and Master's awards commonly have **dissertations** or projects constituting final parts of the programme of study. On occasion, the term *thesis* is used for these pieces of work but that is frequently considered to be incorrect and inappropriate.

Key Words
Dissertation

References
Dunleavy (2003); Murray (2006)

Title

A title is the descriptive name, label or indication of, for example, a book, article, film, **dissertation** or **thesis.**

For a piece of **research**, it is highly significant as it determines the focus, content and scope of a piece of work. Titles work in conjunction with **aims**, **objectives** and **research questions**. Essentially, these should elaborate and develop the arguments and approaches that will respond to the overall title.

A useful technique when thinking of a title is to note all the nouns or 'a name word for things/objects'. For example, in the exemplar title below:

Ticket to Ride: An Investigation into Consumer Behaviour of Commuters on the Mersey Ferry

The key nouns are:

Consumer Behaviour
Commuters
Mersey Ferry

These have a role in directing the work for the study and it might reasonably be anticipated that in terms of literature areas this would need to be examined. In generic terms, consumer behaviour already exists as a clearly defined literature. *Commuters* might also be addressed by this but, together with *Mersey Ferry*, there may well be a need to look at *Transport* or even *Tourism* literature bases to see what they could reveal. This can be done for any title.

When in the process of either conducting or **writing up** a study, it is a good thing to remember to cast an eye back to the title (together with aims, objectives and research questions) in order to check that the study is not drifting off target. Sometimes, when the work is close to being completed, the author might decide that the original title does not really reflect what the work has become. This is not necessarily a problem. On occasion titles are, in effect, *working titles* for what is really a work-in-progress and it is sensible and appropriate to make fine-tuning adjustments to them as the journey of the work becomes more clear.

T

Key Words
Dissertation, Thesis, Writing Up

References
Fisher (2010)

Transcription

Transcription is the process of typing up notes from recordings made of **interviews** and conversations. Transcribing recordings is an essential part of the **research** process. It involves ensuring that verbatim details are written down. By this it is meant that every word, pause, heavy breath, 'um', 'ah' and so on and so forth is noted.

When the transcription process is complete for a piece of research, the transcription documents provide a highly detailed record of all the encounters and interactions that the **researcher(s)** had with **respondent(s)**. By using previously decided approaches to **analysis** (usually outlined in the **research proposal**), researchers can look over the transcripts and begin to make sense and develop findings.

Transcription is a complex and, at times, tediously long process. Assessments on the amount of time required vary but generally 2–3 hours as a minimum for one interview is not unusual. This is something to keep in mind in the **research design** stage. Moreover, when transcribing it is important not to 'correct' anything that the respondent says. This might include grammatical errors, expletives or other informal **language**. This material and its detail are essential to the authenticity of the notes (Bryman and Bell, 2007: 488–91; Wilson, 2010: 256–7).

For a useful illustration of a transcription extract made in the business management and organization sphere, see Wray-Bliss (2004).

Key Words
Analysis, Interview, Research Design, Researcher, Respondent

References
Bryman and Bell (2007); Wilson (2010)

Triangulation

In **research methodology**, the term 'triangulation' means the process whereby a number of methods or sources of **data** are used to double-check and confirm a point, issue or observation (Bryman and Bell, 2007; Gibbert and Ruigrok, 2010; Yauch and Steudel, 2003).

Triangulation can be employed in both **qualitative** and **quantitative** research approaches. Traditionally, it was used in association with positivistic and deductive **research** programmes (see

positivism and **deductivism**). From this perspective, with its focus on **reductionism, objectivity** and **causality**, the purpose therein is to be able to determine in a categorical manner that a particular 'truth' claim is valid and true. In other words, it enhances and confirms the **validity** of the research. All of this seems reasonable and appropriate within a **frame of reference** based on **deductivism**.

Triangulation in relation to **inductivism** and **interpretivism** raises a number of issues and questions. Data gathered through various **methods** within these approaches can work to confirm a particular idea or theme (see **thematic analysis**). For example, an **interview** with a **respondent** can confirm what was recorded as a similar result of a **participant observation**. However, interpretivism has elements of **relativism** and **constructionism,** which means that all data are **context**-related. In other words, there will rarely be a completely categorical 'truth' in a piece of inductive research because this changes to some extent depending on the respondent(s). In relation to triangulation, the question arises, what is actually being triangulated? In other words, the problem or tension runs as follows: in 'purist' and absolutist terms (see **relativism**) if an inductive **researcher** believes that it is difficult, if not impossible, to identify the one answer or truth to an issue – due to context always playing a role – then what would triangulation actually achieve (if indeed it were possible in an interpretivist sense at all)? The answer is that triangulation can play a role but it will be in a different style to the way it is operated in deductive research (that is, **positivism**). In a piece of work using interpretivism, the notion of triangulation merely suggests that different points of view have been collected on the same subject. These do not clearly confirm any 'answer' or specific 'truth', rather they provide further rich data that the researcher can look over and employ to see if a **narrative** (see **narrative research**) or common theme (however broad) is emerging from the data.

Key Words

Causality, Data, Deductivism, Frame of Reference, Inductivism, Reductionism, Relativism, Respondent, Validity

References

Bryman and Bell (2007); Gibbert and Ruigrok (2010); Yauch and Steudel (2003)

Truth

Truth involves that which is considered to be 'true' or a 'fact'. Alternatively expressed, this is similar to saying what is 'accurate', 'good', 'right', and 'valid' and so on and so forth. For deductive approaches to **sense-making**, truth is considered as an objective fact – things are either right or wrong and they fall into a given category or not (see **deductivism** and **objectivity**). In other words, they are true and valid for that particular belief system, **theory**, classification or categorization. Approaches espousing inductive and subjective views of truth see it as being less categorical (see **inductivism** and **subjectivity**). Somebody who makes sense of the world using a deductive, positivistic methodology would not see notions of truth in the same manner that a person employing a postmodern or post-structuralist perspective would (see **deductivism**, **positivism**, **postmodernism** and **poststructuralism**) (Al-Amoudi, 2007).

Truth, to a certain degree, is a view, a perspective or a point of view. For example, even a seemingly categorical event such as a road accident may elicit differing points of view on what occurred. Truth is made or constructed (or not) based on the given (or shifting) **contexts** and philosophical perspectives adhered to. However, in questioning and challenging the notion of truth, we must be careful not to slip into forms of **relativism**. In their most extreme forms, relativist statements on tragic or controversial issues can seem highly insulting and insensitive. An example of such an unacceptable act would be, for example, denial or challenging of the truth of genocide and Holocaust in the Second World War or suggesting that it was not as horrific as it actually was. There are individuals who have done such acts (see the case, for example, of the British writer David Irving) but this has led some countries to make Holocaust denial against their national laws.

Key Words
Inductivism, Deductivism, Objectivity, Positivism, Postmodernism, Sense-making, Subjectivity

References
Al-Amoudi (2007)

Validity

In **research**, validity concerns the degree to which a piece of research manages to portray, and to respond to, its **objectives** and the **concepts** it set out to consider or measure in as accurate and insightful manner as possible. In other words, did the research achieve what it set out to do and can its findings be believed; are they a credible account of the issues and situation that were being looked at?

Validity techniques and approaches will vary depending on the inductive and deductive orientation of the **research methodology** being employed (see **inductivism** and **deductivism**) and may to some greater or lesser extent involve some form of **triangulation** (Cameron and Price, 2009: 216–18).

Key Words
Objectives, Triangulation

References
Cameron and Price (2009)

Variables

More often than not, **research** is interested in, and concentrates its attention on, particular types or kinds of **data**. These pieces of data are commonly referred to as variables. Variables can measure a wide range of aspects including attributes, opinions, behaviours, number of occurrences of an event and so on and so forth. *Behaviour variables*, as the name suggests, try to gauge how people behave or conduct themselves. Behaviour variables record what **researchers** or participants actually do during the course of the research investigation.

Key Words
Data, Variables

References
Saunders, Lewis and Thornhill (2007)

V

Weltanschauung

This is a term that is derived from philosophy. It means 'world view' and points at the cumulative totality of the way people view the world. Although many people may share perspectives, it is likely that each person will have a unique and individual mind-set and collection of ideas, opinions, experiences and perspectives that go to make up his or her 'world view'. This means that any given person's *Weltanschauung* may well be full of subjectivity.

The notion of a world view is an important one for research methodology because any chosen methodology has to decide how it will address and treat the issue of people's world view. For inductive approaches (see **inductivism**), the research design will be keen to try to describe the respondent's position in as full and as rich a way as possible. The subjectivity inherent in a world view will be embraced and analysed. For deductive approaches, the idea of a wide range of differing world views being in operation may be seen as a variation that needs to be addressed in an as objective manner as possible. The aim here will be to try to ensure that bias is not allowed to enter the research project.

Key Words
Experience, Objectivity, Opinion, Perspective, Subjectivity

References
Bell and Taylor (2004); Tadajewski (2009)

Writing Up

Writing up is the act and process of **researcher(s)** committing to paper, in the form of a project, **dissertation** or **thesis**, the **research** 'story'. All the general structure of the document is likely to follow is an approximately standard format. It will require different **language** and layout depending on whether or not it is, for example, an inductivistic, interpretivistic work or a deductive, positivistic project (see **inductivism, interpretivism, deductivism**, and **positivism**). Moreover, different **research methods** and techniques will have their own protocols and layouts (see for example **case study**). Wilson (2010: 271–99) makes a number of useful and apposite comments to keep in mind when writing. These include, for example

- tackling the challenge of where to start
- the idea of drawing up a writing timetable
- issues of writing style, sentence length, sexism, **referencing** and political correctness
- important matters of **ethics** and **confidentiality**
- the importance of developing an argument (and avoiding simply describing)

There are also submission format and regulations and the possibility of publishing some or all of your work and the follow-on from the write-up (see also Fisher, 2010; Wolcott, 2009).

A useful tip for the writing-up phase is the notion of 'chunk and chip'. This means chop the overall dissertation or thesis task into bite-sized or manageable portions. One guideline here is to think about what you could do in a thirty-minute or hour free slot. This is an important idea because quite often the free time we have does not present itself in big slabs of available time. Tackling the write-up this way means that, in addition to the big scheduled periods of writing or work, you can also 'chip away' at the overall task gradually. This all helps move you slowly 'up the mountain'. This technique also allows you to tackle parts of the dissertation or thesis and remain relatively fresh. One of the dangers of tackling something like writing up research, be it a dissertation, thesis or paper, is that researchers/students become exhausted and bogged down. 'Chunk and chip' is a small technique to try and avoid this.

Key Words
Dissertation, Language, Thesis

References
Fisher (2010); Wilson (2010); Wolcott (2009)

References and Bibliography

Abrams, L. (2010) 'Sampling "hard to reach" populations in qualitative research: The case of incarcerated youth', *Qualitative Social Work*, 9(4): 536–50.

Ackermann, F., Eden, C. and Brown, I. (2005) *The Practice of Making Strategy*, London: Sage Publications.

Ackroyd, S. and Fleetwood, S. (2001) *Realist Perspectives on Organization and Management*, London: Routledge.

Aguinas, H., Pierce, C., Bosco, F. and Muslin, I. (2008) 'First decade of organizational research methods: Trends in design, measurement and data-analysis topics', *Organizational Research Methods*, 12(1): 69–112.

Ailon, G. (2006) 'What B would otherwise do: A critique of conceptualizations of power in organization theory', *Organization*, 13(6): 771–800.

Al-Amoudi, I. (2007) 'Redrawing Foucault's social ontology', *Organization*, 14(4): 543–63.

Allan, K. (2010) *Contemporary Social and Sociological Theory: Visualizing Social Worlds*, London: Sage Publications.

Allard-Poesi, F. (2005) 'The paradox of sensemaking in organizational analysis', *Organization*, 12(2): 169–96.

Alvesson, M. and Deetz, S. (2000) *Doing Critical Management Research*, London: Sage Publications.

Alvesson, M. and Sköldberg, K. (2009) *Reflexive Methodology, New Vistas in Qualitative Research*, London: Sage Publications.

Alvesson, M. and Willmott, H. (1992) *Critical Management Studies*, London: Sage Publications.

Alvesson, M. and Willmott, H. (1996) *Making Sense of Management: A Critical Introduction*, London: Sage Publications.

Armstrong, K. (1999) 'Nike's communication with black audiences: A sociological analysis of advertising effectiveness via Symbolic Interactionism', *Journal of Sports and Social Issues*, 23(3): 266–86.

Behling, O. and Law, K. (2000) *Translating Questionnaires and Other Research Instruments: Problems and Solutions*, Thousand Oaks, CA: Sage Publications.

Bell, E. and Taylor, E. (2004) 'From outward bound to inward bound: The prophetic voices and discursive practices of spiritual management development', *Human Relations*, 57(4): 439–66.

Berger, P. and Luckmann, T. (1966) *The Social Construction of Reality: A Treatise in the Sociology of Knowledge*, London: Penguin.

Bergström, O. and Knights, D. (2006) 'Organizational discourse and subjectivity: subjectification during processes of recruitment', *Human Relations*, 59(3): 351–77.

Bhaskar, R. (1989) *The Possibility of Naturalism*, Hemel Hempstead: Harvester Wheatsheaf.

Biggam, J. (2008) *Succeeding With Your Master's* Dissertation: *A Step-By-Step Handbook*, Milton Keynes: Open University Press.

Böhm, S. and Batta, A. (2010) 'Just doing it: Enjoying commodity fetishism with Lacan', *Organization,* 17(3): 345–61.

Boje, D. (2001) *Narrative Methods for Organizational and Communication Research*, London: Sage Publications.

Bold, C. (2011) *Using Narrative in Research*, London: Sage Publications.

Brar, B. (2003) 'SAARC: If functionalism has failed, will realism work?', *South Asian Survey*, 10(1): 31–41.

Brewis, J. (2005) 'Signing my life away? Researching sex and organization', *Organization*, 12 (4): 493–510.

Broussine, M. (2008) *Creative Methods in Organizational Research*, London: Sage Publications.

Bulmer, M. (2008) 'The Ethics of Social Research' in Gilbert, N. (2008) *Researching Social Life*, London: Sage Publications, pp. 45–57.

Bryman, A. and Bell, E. (2007) *Business Research Methods*, Oxford: Oxford University Press.

Bryman, A. (2008) *Social Research Methods*, Oxford: Oxford University Press.

Buchanan, D. and Bryman, A. (2007) 'Contextualising methods choice in organizational research', *Organizational Research Methods*, 10(3): 483–501.

Bulmer, M. (2012) *Questionnaires 2 (Four Volume Set)*, London: Sage Publications.

Burrell, G. and Morgan, G. (1979) *Sociological Paradigms and Organizational Analysis*, Oxford: Heinemann Educational Ltd.

Cameron, S. and Price, D. (2009) *Business Research Methods: A Practical Approach*, London: CIPD.

Casey, C. (2004) 'Bureaucracy re-enchanted? Spirit, experts and authority in organizations', *Organization*, 11(1): 59–79.

Cassell, C. and Symon, G. (2004) *Essential Guide to Qualitative Methods in Organizational Research*, London: Sage Publications.

Chang, H. (2008) *Autoethnography as Method (Developing Qualitative Inquiry)*, Walnut Creek, CA: Left Coast Press Inc.

Chapman, S. and McNeill, P. (2005) *Research Methods: Textbook*, London: Routledge.

Charmaz, K. (2006) *Consulting Grounded Theory: A Practical Guide Through Qualitative Analysis*, London: Sage Publications.

Chia, R. (1996) *Organizational Analysis as Deconstructive Practice*, Berlin: Walter de Gruyter and Co.

Clark, P. and Creswell, J. (2008) *The Mixed Methods Reader*, Thousand Oaks, CA: Sage Publications.

Clegg, S., Kornberger, M. and Pitsis, T. (2008) *Managing and Organizations: An Introduction to Theory and Practice*, London: Sage Publications.

Collis, J. and Hussey, R. (2009) *Business Research: A Practical Guide for Undergraduate and Postgraduate Students*, Basingstoke: Palgrave Macmillan.

Contu, A. and Willmott, H. (2005) 'You spin me round: The realist turn in organization and management studies', *Journal of Management Studies*, 42(8): 1645–62.

Contu, A., Driver, M. and Jones, C. (2010) 'Jacques Lacan and organization studies' special issue of *Organization*, 17(3): 307–410.

Cooper, B. (1989) 'Modernism, postmodernism and organizational analysis 3: the contribution of Jacques Derrida', *Organization Studies*, 10(4): 479–502.

Cooke, B. and Wolfram Cox, J. (2005) *Fundamentals of Action Research*, London: Sage Publications.

Cooper, H. (2009) *Research Synthesis and Meta-Analysis*, London: Sage Publications.

Couvalis, G. (1997) *The Philosophy of Science*, London: Sage Publications.

Creswell, J. and Clark, P. (2010) *Designing and Conducting Mixed Methods Research*, Thousand Oaks, CA: Sage Publications.

Curwin, J. and Slater, R. (2007) *Quantitative Methods: A Short Course*, London: Thomson Learning.

Czarniawska, B. (1998) *A Narrative Approach in Organization Studies*, Thousand Oaks, CA: Sage Publications.

Czarniawska, B. (2002) *A Tale of Three Cities or the Glocalization of City Management*, Oxford: Oxford University Press.

Czarniawska, B. (2003) *Narratives We Organize By*, Amsterdam: John Benjamins.

Czarniawska, B. (2004) *Narratives in Social Science Research*, London: Sage Publications.

Dahl, D., Mo, Q. and Vannucci, M. (2008) 'Simultaneous inference for multiple testing and clustering via a Dirichlet process mixture model', *Statistical Modelling*, 8(1): 23–9.

Denzin, N. (2008) *Collecting and Interpreting Qualitative Materials*, London: Sage Publications.

Denzin, N. and Lincoln, Y. (2008) *The Landscape of Qualitative Research*, London: Sage Publications.

Dereli, C. and Stokes, P. (2008) 'Exploring the tension between the scientific and the spiritual in the Age of Modernism: Implications for management theory in the era of postmodernity', *Philosophy of Management*, 6(3): 52–67.

Derrida, J. (1973) *Speech and Phenomena and Other Essays on Husserl's Theory of Signs*, Evanston: Northwestern University Press.

Derrida, J. (1976) *Of Grammatology*, Baltimore: John Hopkins University Press.

Di Maggio, P. J. and Powell, W. W. (2002) 'The iron cage revisited: institutional isomorphism and collective rationality in organizational fields', in Clegg, S. (ed.) *Central Currents in Organizational Studies I Frameworks and Applications Vol 3.*, London: Sage Publications, pp. 324–62.

Donaldson, L. (1996) *For Positivist Organization Theory*, London: Sage Publications.

Donaldson, L. (2005) 'Vita contemplative: Following the scientific method – how I became a committed functionalist and positivist', *Organization Studies*, 26(7): 1071–88.

Draucker, C., Martsoff, D., Ross, R. and Rusk, T. (2007) 'Theoretical Sampling and Category Development in Grounded Theory', *Qualitative Health Research*, 21(2): 1137–48.

Driver, M. (2008) 'Every bite you take ... food and the struggles of embodies subjectivity in organizations', *Human Relations*, 61(7): 913–34.

Du Gay, P. and Elliott, A. (2008) *Identity in Question*, London: Sage Publications.

Dundon, T. and Ryan, P. (2010) 'Interviewing reluctant respondents: Strikes, henchmen and Gaelic games', *Organizational Research Methods*, 13(3): 562–81.

Dunleavy, P. (2003) *Authoring a PhD*, Basingstoke: Palgrave Macmillan.

Easterby-Smith, M., Thorpe, R. and Jackson, P. (2008) *Management Research: Theory and Practice*, London: Sage Publications.

Eastmond, M. (2007) 'Stories as lived experience: Narratives in forced migration research', *Journal of Refugee Studies*, 20(2): 248–64.

Eden, C. and Huxham, C. (1996) 'Action research for management research', *British Journal of Management*, 7(1): 75–86.

Ellis, N. (2008) 'What the hell is that? The representation of professional service markets in The Simpsons', *Organization*, 15(5): 705–23.

Eriksson, P. and Kovalainen, A. (2008) *Qualitative Methods in Business Research*, London: Sage Publication.

Erola, J. (2010) 'Why probability has not succeeded in sociology', *Sociology*, 44(1): 121–38.

Fairclough, N. (2005) 'Discourse analysis in organization studies: The case for critical realism', *Organization Studies*, 26(6): 915–39.

Fairclough, N. (2010) *Critical Discourse Analysis: The Critical Study of Language*, Harlow: Pearson Education Ltd.

Fairhurst, G. (2004) 'Textuality and agency in interaction analysis', *Organization*, 11(3): 335–53.

Farnsworth, J. and Boon, B. (2010) 'Analysing group dynamics within the focus group', *Qualitative Research*, 10(5): 605–24.

Fineman, S., Gabriel, Y. and Sims, D. (2010) *Organizing and Organizations*, London: Sage Publications.

Fink, A. (2009) *Conducting Research Literature Reviews: From the Internet to Paper*, London: Sage Publications.

Fisher, C. (2010) *Researching and Writing a Dissertation: A Guidebook for Business Students*, London: FT/Prentice Hall.

Fleetwood, S. (2005) 'The ontology of organization and management studies: A critical realist approach', *Organization*, 12(2): 197–222.

Fleetwood, S. and Ackroyd, S. (2004) *Critical Realist Applications in Organization and Management Studies*, London: Routledge.

Ford, J. and Harding, N. (2008) 'Fear and loathing in Harrogate, or a study of a conference', *Organization*, 15(2): 233–50.

Fowler, F. (2008) *Survey Research Methods*, Thousand Oaks, CA: Sage Publications.

Gabriel, Y. (2000) *Storytelling in Organizations*, Oxford: Oxford University Press.

Gabriel, Y. (2004) *Myths, Stories and Organizations: Premodern Narratives for Our Times*, Oxford: Oxford University Press.

Gelbrich, K. and Roschk, H. (2011) 'A meta-analysis of organizational complaint handling and customer responses', *Journal of Service Research*, 14(1): 24–43.

Ghaye, T. and Lillyman, S. (2008) *Learning Journals and Critical Incidents: Reflective Practice for Health Care Professionals*, London: Mark Allen Publishing.

Gibbert, M. and Ruigrok, W. (2010) 'The "what" and "how" of case study rigour: three strategies based on published work', *Organizational Research Methods*, 13(4): 710–37.

Gill, J. and Johnson, P. (2010) *Research Methods for Managers*, London: Sage Publications.

Glaser, B. and Strauss, A. (1967) *The Discovery of Grounded Theory: Strategies for Qualitative Research*, Chicago, IL: Aldine Publishing Company.

Goulding, C. (2002) *Grounded Theory: A Practical Guide for Management, Business and Market Researchers*, London: Sage Publications.

Grant, D., Hardy, C., Oswick, C. and Putnam, L. (2004) *The Sage Handbook of Organizational Discourse*, London: Sage Publications.

Grant, D., Hardy, C. and Putnam, L. (eds) (2011a) *Organizational Discourse Studies Volume I: Theoretical Developments*, London: Sage Publications.

Grant, D., Hardy, C. and Putnam, L. (eds) (2011b) *Organizational Discourse Studies Volume II: Methods*, London: Sage Publications.

Grant, D., Hardy, C. and Putnam, L. (eds) (2011c) *Organizational Discourse Studies Volume III: Applications and Contexts*, London: Sage Publications.

Greetham, B. (2009) *How to Write Your Undergraduate Dissertation*, Basingstoke: Palgrave Macmillan.

(Van) Gregg, R. (2011) *Research Methods in Practice: Strategies for Description and Causation*, Thousand Oaks, CA: Sage Publications.

Ha, R. (2011) *Integrative Statistics for the Social and Behavioural Sciences*, London: Sage Publications.

Hair, J., Money, A., Samouel, P. and Page M. (2007) *Research Methods for Business*, Chichester: John Wiley and Sons.

Halkier, B. (2010) 'Focus Groups as social enactments: integrating interaction and content in the analysis of focus group data', *Qualitative Research*, 10(1): 71–89.

Hammersley, M. (2011) *Methodology: Who Needs It?* London: Sage Publications.

Hancock, P. (2005) 'Uncovering the semiotic in organizational aesthetics', *Organization*, 12(1): 29–50.

Hansen, H. (2006) 'The ethnonarrative approach', *Human Relations*, 59(8): 1049–75.

Hardy, C. (2004) 'Scaling up and bearing down in discourse analysis: Questions regarding textual agencies and their content', *Organization*, 11(3): 415–25.

Hart, C. (1998) *Doing a Literature Review: Releasing the Social Science Research Imagination*, London: Sage Publications.

Hart, C. (2004) *Doing Your Masters Dissertation*, London: Sage Publications.

Hickey, L. (1993) 'Stylistics, pragmatics and pragmastylistics', *Revue Belge de Philologie and Pragmastylistics*, 71(71–3): 573–86.

Hickey, L. and Stewart, M. (2005) *Politeness in Europe*, Ontario: Multilingual Matters Ltd.

Hultsch, D., MacDonald, S., Hunter, M., Maitland, S. and Dixon, R. (2002) 'Sampling and generalisability in developmental research: Comparison of random and convenience sample of older adults', *International Journal of Behavioral Development*, 26(4): 345–59.

Humphreys, M., Brown, A. and Hatch, M. (2003) 'Is ethnography jazz?' *Organization*, 10(1): 5–31.

Hunt, S. and Ruiz Junco, N. (2006) 'Introduction to two thematic issues: Defective memory and analytical autoethnography', *Journal of Contemporary Ethnography*, 35(4): 371–2 (and the subsequent articles in the special issue).

Israel, M. and Hay, I. (2006) *Research Ethics for Social Scientists*, London: Sage Publications.

Jankowicz, A. (2005) *Business Research Projects*, London: Thompson Learning.

Jehn, K. (1993) 'Hapax Legomenon II: Theory, a Thesaurus, and Word Frequency', *Field Methods*, 5(1): 8–10.

Jehn, K. (2010) 'A multi-method approach to the study of sensitive organizational issues', *Journal of Mixed Methods* Research, 4(4): 313–41.

Jensen, A. (2007) *Theological Hermeneutics*, London: SCM Press.

Jesson, J. and Matheson, L. (2011) *Doing Your Literature Review: Traditional and Systematic Techniques*, London: Sage Publications.

Johnsen, R. and Gudmand-Høyer, M. (2010) 'Lacan and the lack of humanity in HRM', *Organization*, May 17(3): 331–44.

Jones, C. (2004) 'Jacques Derrida', in S. Linstead (ed.) *Organization Theory and Postmodern Thought*, London: Sage Publications, pp. 34–63.

Jones, C. (2007) 'Friedman with Derrida', *Business and Society Review*, 112(4): 511–32.

Jones, C. (2010) 'Derrida, business, ethics', special issue of *Business Ethics: A European Review*, 19(3): 233–305.

Jones, C., Parker, M. and Ten Bos, R. (2005) *For Business Ethics*, London: Routledge.

Kerssens-van Drongelen, I. (2001) 'The iterative theory-building process: rationale, principles and evaluation', *Management Decision*, 39(7): 503–12.

King, N. and Horrocks, C. (2010) *Interviews in Qualitative Research*, London: Sage Publications.

Kirkpatrick, I. and Ackroyd, S. (2003) 'Archetype theory and the changing professional organization: A critique and alternative', *Organization*, 10(4): 731–50.

Knights, D. and Willmott, H. (1999) *Management Lives*, London: Sage Publications.

Knights, D. (2002) 'Writing Organizational Analysis into Foucault', *Organization*, 9(4): 575–93.

Kolar, T. and Kolar, I. (2008) 'What respondents really expect from researchers', *Evaluation Review*, 32(4): 363–91.

Kremelberg, D. (2011) *Practical Statistics*, Thousand Oaks, CA: Sage Publications.

Kuhn, T. (1970) *The Structure of Scientific Revolutions*, Chicago: University of Chicago Press.

Kuhn, T. (2009) 'Positioning lawyers: discursive resources, professional ethics and identification', *Organization*, 16(5): 681–704.

Kvale, S. (2007) *Doing Interviews*, London: Sage Publications.

Lam, T., Green, K. and Bordignon, C. (2002) 'Effects of item grouping and position of the 'Don't Know' option on questionnaire response; *Field Methods*, 14(4): 65–87.

Lee, B. and Cassell, C. (2011) *Challenges and Controversies in Management Research*, London: Routledge.

Lincoln, Y. and Guba, E. (1985) *Naturalistic Enquiry*, Thousand Oaks, CA: Sage Publications.

Linstead, S. and Brewis, J. (2007) 'Passion, knowledge and motivation: Ontologies of desire', *Organization*, 14(3): 351–71.

Linstead, S., Fulop, L. and Lilley, S. (2009) *Management and Organization: A Critical Text*, Basingstoke: Palgrave Macmillan.

LoConto, D. and Jones-Pruett, L. (2006) 'The influence of Charles A Ellwood on Herbert Blumer and Symbolic Interactionism', *Journal of Classical Sociology*, 6(1): 75–99.

Lundgren, D. (2005) 'Handbook of Symbolic Interactionism', *Contemporary Sociology: A Journal of Reviews*, 34(3): 327–9.

Lux, S., Crook, R. and Woehr, D. (2011) 'Mixing business with politics: A meta-analysis of the antecedents and outcomes of corporate political activity', *Journal of Management*, 37(1): 223–47.

Malpas, S. and Wake, P. (2006) *The Routledge Companion to Critical Theory*, London: Routledge.

Martens, W. (2006) 'The distinctions within organizations: Luhmann from a cultural perspective', *Organization*, 13(1): 83–108.

Maylor, H. and Blackmon, K. (2005) *Researching Business and Management*, Basingstoke: Palgrave Macmillan.

McCabe, D. (2007) 'Individualization at work? Subjectivity, teamworking and anti-unionism', *Organization*, 14(2): 243–66.

McKenna, E. (2000) *Business Psychology and Organisational Behaviour*, Hove: Psychology Press Ltd.

Meade, A., Michels, L. and Lautenschlager, G. (2007) 'Are internet and paper-and-pencil tests truly comparable? An experimental design measurement invariance study', *Organizational Research Methods*, 10(2): 322–45.

Menard, S. (2007) *Handbook of Longitudinal Research*, Amsterdam: Elsevier.

Mescher, S., Benschop, Y. and Doorewaard, H. (2010) 'Representations of work: life balance support', *Human Relations*, 63(1): 21–39.

Miettinen, R. and Virkkunen, J. (2005) 'Epistemic objects, artefacts and organizational change', *Organization*, 12(3): 437–56.

Monahan, T. and Fisher, J. (2010) 'Benefits of 'observer effects': lessons from the field', *Qualitative Research*, 10(3): 357–76.

Muncey, T. (2010) *Creating Autoethnographies*, London/CA: Sage Publications.

Murray, R. (2006) *How to Write a Thesis*, Maidenhead: Open University Press/McGraw Hill.

Mutch, A. (2005) 'Discussion of Willmott: Critical Realism, agency and discourse – moving the debate forward', *Organization*, 12(5): 781–6.

Nichols, E. and Hunter-Childs, J. (2009) 'Respondent debriefings conducted by experts: A technique for questionnaire evaluation', *Field Methods*, 21(2): 115–32.

O'Doherty, D. (2008) 'The blur sensation: Shadows of the future', *Organization*, 15(4): 535–61.

Oliver, P. (2010) *The Student's Guide to Research Ethics*, Maidenhead: Open University Press.

Payne, G. (2011) *Teaching Quantitative Methods: Getting the Basics Rights*, London: Sage Publications.

Perrow, C. (2008) 'Conservative radicalism', *Organization*, 15(6): 915–21.

Phillips, E. and Pugh, D. (2010) *How to get a PhD: A Handbook for Students and Their Supervisors*, London: McGraw-Hill Education/Open University Press.

Phillips, N., Sewell, G. and Jaynes, S. (2008) 'Applying critical discourse analysis in strategic management research', *Organizational Research Methods*, 11(4): 770–89.

Pilarski, A. (2011) 'The past and future of Feminist biblical hermeneutics', *Biblical Theology Bulletin: A Journal of Bible and Theology*, 41(1): 16–23.

Plowright, D. (2010) *Using Mixed Methods: Frameworks for An Integrated Technology*, London: Sage Publications.

Polonsky, M. and Waller, D. (2011) *Designing and Managing a Research Project*, Thousand Oaks, CA: Sage Publications.

Prasad, A. (2002) 'The contest over meaning: Hermeneutics as an interpretive methodology for understanding texts', *Organizational Research Methods*, 5(1): 12–33.

Quinton, S. and Smallbone, T. (2006) *Postgraduate Research in Business: A Critical Guide*, London: Sage Publications.

Raimond, P. (1993) *Management Projects: Design, Research and Presentation*, London: Chapman Hall.

Raleigh-Yow, V. (1994) *Recording Oral History*, London: Sage Publications.

Reason, P. and Bradbury, H. (2001) (eds) *Handbook of Action Research: Participative Inquiry and Practice*, London: Sage Publications.

Reed, M. (2005) 'Reflections on the realist turn in organization and management studies', *British Journal of Management Studies*, 42(8): 1621–44.

Remler, D. and Van Ryzin, G. (2011) *Research Methods in Practice: Strategies for Description and Causation*, Thousand Oaks, CA: Sage Publications.

Ridley, D. (2008) *The Literature Review: a Step-by-Step Guide for Students*, London: Sage Publications.

Riley, J. (1990) *Getting the Most from your Data: A Handbook of Practical Ideas on How to Analyse Data*, London, Technical and Educational Services Ltd.

Rhodes, C. and Brown, A. (2005) 'Writing responsibly: Narrative fiction and organization studies', *Organization*, 12(4): 467–91.

Robertson, M. and Swan, J. (2004) 'Going public: The emergence and effects of soft-bureaucracy within a knowledge-intensive firm', *Organization*, 11(1): 123–48.

Roethlisberger, F. and Dickson, W. (1939) *Management and the Worker*, Cambridge, MA: Harvard University Press.

Rosenthal, P. and Peccei, R. (2006) 'The social construction of clients by service agents in reformed welfare administration', *Human Relations*, 59(12): 1633–58.

Saldaña, J. (2009) *The Coding Manual for Qualitative Researchers*, London: Sage Publications.

Sapsford, R. (2006) *Data Collection and Analysis*, London: Sage Publications.

Saunders, M., Lewis, P. and Thornhill, A. (2007) *Research Methods for Business Students*, London: FT/Prentice Hall.

Silverman, D. (2006) *Interpreting Qualitative Data: Methods for Analyzing Talk, Text and Interaction*, London: Sage Publications.

Silverman, D. (2010a) *Doing Qualitative Research*, London: Sage Publications.

Silverman, D. (2010b) *Qualitative Research*, London: Sage Publications.

Sim, S. and Van Loon, B. (2005) *Introducing Critical Theory*, Royston: Icon Books Ltd.

Sims, D., Pullen, A. and Beech, N. (2007) *Exploring Identity: Concepts and Methods*, Basingstoke: Palgrave Macmillan.

Spector, P. and Brannich, M. (2010) 'Common methods issues: An Introduction to the feature topic in organizational research methods', *Organizational Research Methods*, 13(3): 403–6.

Spender, J. and Scherer, A. (2007) 'The philosophical foundation of knowledge management: editors' introduction', *Organization*, 14(1): 5–28.

Steinberg, W. (2010) *Statistics Alive!* London: Sage Publications.

Stokes, P. and McCulloch, A. (2006) 'Beyond the Doctoral Process: A Call for the Re-focusing of the "How to...Get a PhD Literature"', *Journal of Graduate Education*, 3(4) Autumn, pp. 107–15.

Stovall, S. (2010) 'Recreating the Arsenal of Venice: Using experiential activities to teach the history of management', *Journal of Management Education*, 34(3): 458–73.

Strauss, A. and Corbin, J. (1998) *Basics of Qualitative Research*, Thousand Oaks, CA: Sage Publications.

Swift, L. and Piff, S. (2010) *Quantitative Methods for Business, Management and Finance*, Basingstoke: Palgrave Macmillan.

Tadajewski, M. (2009) 'The debate that won't die? Values incommensurability, antagonism and theory choice', *Organization*, 16(4): 467–85.

Taylor, J. and Robichaud, D. (2004) 'Finding the organization in the communication: Discourse as action and sensemaking', *Organization*, 11(3): 393–413.

Tietze, S., Cohen, L. and Musson, G. (2003) *Understanding Organizations Through Language*, London: Sage Publications.

Thody, A. (2006) *Writing and Presenting Research*, London: Sage Publications.

Thompson, P. (1993) 'Postmodernism: Fatal Distraction', in Hassard, J. and Parker, M. *Postmodernism and Organizations*, London: Sage Publications, pp. 183–203.

Tripp, D. (1993) *Critical Incidents in Teaching: Developing Professional Judgement*, London: Routledge.

Van Maanen, J. (1988) *Tales of the Field: On Writing Ethnography*, Chicago: University of Chicago Press.

Van Maanen, J. (2010) 'A song for my support: more tales of the field', *Organizational Research Methods*, 13(2): 240–55.

Waddington, D. (2004) 'Participant Observation', in Cassell, C. and Symon, G. *Essential Guide to Qualitative Methods in Organizational Research*, London: Sage Publications, pp. 165–79.

Walden, J. (2009) 'A guide to writing the dissertation literature review', *Practical Assessment, Research & Evaluation*, 14(13): 1–13, June.

Wallgren, A. (1996) *Graphing Statistics and Data*, London: Sage Publications.

Watson, T. and Harris, P. (1999) *The Emergent Manager*, London: Sage Publications.

Watson, T. (2006) *Management and Organization*, Basingstoke: Palgrave Macmillan.

Weick, K. (1995) *Sensemaking in Organizations*, London: Sage Publications.

Weick, K. (2001) *Making Sense of the Organization*, Oxford: Oxford University Press.

Whitley, R. (2003) 'From the search for universal correlations to the institutional structuring of economic organization and change: The development and future of organization studies', *Organization*, 10(3): 481–501.

Whittle, A. (2008) 'From flexibility to work-life balance: Exploring the changing discourses of management consultants', *Organization*, 15(4): 513–34.

Willmott, H. (2005) 'Theorizing contemporary control: Some poststructuralist responses to some critical realist questions', *Organization*, 12(5): 747–80.

Willis, J. (2007) *Foundations of Qualitative Research*, Thousand Oaks, CA: Sage Publications.

Wilson, J. (2010) *Essentials of Business Research: A Guide to Doing Your Research Project*, London: Sage Publications.

Wilson, J. (Prof) and Toms, S. (2010) 'In defence of business history: A reply to Taylor, Bell and Cooke', *Management and Organizational History*, 5: 109–20.

Wolcott, F. (2009) *Writing Up Qualitative Research*, Thousand Oaks, CA: Sage Publications.

Wolfram Cox, J. and Hassard, J. (2005) 'Triangulation in organizational research: A re-presentation', *Organization*, 12(1): 109–33.

Woods, C. (2007) 'Empirical histograms in item response theory with ordinal data', *Educational and Psychological Measurement*, 67(1): 73–87.

Wootton, S. and Horne, T. (2002) *'Thinking skills for Managers: Managers as Thoughtful People*, London: Libra House Ltd.

Woźniak, A. (2010) 'The dream that caused reality: The place of the Lacanian subject of science in the field of organization', *Organization*, May 17(3): 395–411.

Wray-Bliss, E. (2002) 'Abstract ethics, embodied ethics: the strange marriage of Foucault and positivism in LPT', *Organization*, 9(1): 5–39.

Wray-Bliss, E. (2004) 'The right to respond? The monopolisation of "Voice" in CMS', *Ephemera*, 4(2): 101–20.

Wray-Bliss, E. and Brewis, J. (2008), 'Re-searching ethics: towards a more reflexive Critical Management Studies', *Organization Studies*, 29(12): 1521–40.

Wright, D. and London, K. (2009) *Modern Regression Techniques Using R*, London: Sage Publications.

Yauch, C. and Steudel, H. (2003) 'Complementary use of qualitative and quantitative cultural assessment methods', *Organizational Research Methods*, 6(4): 465–81.

Yin, R. K. (2002) *Case Study Research: Design and Methods*, London: Sage Publications.

Yin, R. K. (2011) *Applications of Case Study Research*, London: Sage Publications.

Zhang, Z., Spicer, A. and Hancock, P. (2008) 'Hyper-organizational space in the work of J.G.Ballard', *Organization*: 15(6): 889–910.

Index

covert research 28–9
critical incident method (CIM) 29
critical management studies
  (CMS) 29–30, 34, 45, 101
critical realism 30–1, 92
Critical Theory 29, 31

data 32, 60, 131
  continuous 56
  qualitative 19, 60–1
  quantitative 19, 60
  see also variables
data collection 4, 33, 52, 112, 116
deconstructionism 33–4
deductivism 34–5, 47, 59, 92,
  115
  analysis 7
  bias 14
  causality 17
  generalizability 51
  knowledge 65
  linearity 69
  mixed methods 80–1
  reflexivity 109
  and subjectivity 123
  triangulation 128–9
  truth 130
  see also positivism
Deleuze, G. 101
Delphi technique 35–6
Derrida, J. 33, 101
Descartes, R. 83
determinism 36–7, 47, 100
Dickson, W. 54
Diderot, D. 83
discourse 37, 67
discourse analysis 34, 37, 102
discrete data 32
discursive practices 37
discussion 38, 39
dissertations 1, 38–9, 126
distribution 39
  bimodal 82

  normal 86–7
  skewed 86
Duchamp, M. 83

Eden, C. 3
emic accounts 40, 45
empiricism 40–1
Enlightenment 83
epistemology 41–3, 49, 65,
  99–100, 113
ethics 2, 8, 21, 28, 43–4, 116, 118
ethics committees 21, 43
ethnography 11, 44–5, 96, 123
etic accounts 40, 45–6
European Group on
  Organizational Studies (EGOS)
  30
evaluation 46
executive summary of a report 2
experimental design 17, 26–7, 40,
  46–7, 94

Fisher, C. 22, 117
focus groups 48–9
Foucault, M. 101
frame of reference 45, 49–50
Frankfurt School 31
frequency 14, 50
frequency table 50
Fromm, E. 31
functionalism 50
functionalist paradigm 95

generalizability 46, 51–2
Gestalt 49
Glaser, B. 52
Goulding, C. 52
Grounded Theory 12, 19, 23,
  52–3, 126

Habermas, J. 31
Harvard Referencing Format
  107–8